"I need a little time alone, Mike.

To think about things." As soon as she'd spoken, Lisa wished she could recall the words. She could tell from his expression that she'd hurt him.

"I see. What you're saying is that you'd like me to leave."

"No, I . . ."

"Oh, yes, you . . ." he mocked. "It's a kid's way to handle things, Lisa. Adults stay and talk things out. If you want loneliness and silence, you've got it."

He walked out of the room, and in a minute she heard the front door slam.

Dear Reader,

When two people fall in love, the world is suddenly new and exciting, and it's that same excitement we bring to you in Silhouette Intimate Moments. These are stories with scope, with grandeur. These characters lead the lives we all dream of, and everything they do reflects the wonder of being in love.

Longer and more sensuous than most romances, Silhouette Intimate Moments novels take you away from everyday life and let you share the magic of love. Adventure, glamour, drama, even suspense—these are the passwords that let you into a world where love has a power beyond the ordinary, where the best authors in the field today create stories of love and commitment that will stay with you always.

In coming months look for novels by your favorite authors: Maura Seger, Parris Afton Bonds, Elizabeth Lowell and Erin St. Claire, to name just a few. And whenever you buy books, look for all the Silhouette Intimate Moments, love stories *for* today's women *by* today's women.

Leslie J. Wainger
Senior Editor
Silhouette Books

IMRL-7/85

America's Publisher of Contemporary Romance

SILHOUETTE BOOKS
300 E. 42nd St., New York, N.Y. 10017

Distributed by Pocket Books

ISBN: 0-373-07116-7

First Silhouette Books printing October 1985

10 9 8 7 6 5 4 3 2 1

America's Publisher of Contemporary Romance

Printed in the U.S.A.

Books by Pat Wallace

Silhouette Special Edition

Silver Fire #56
My Loving Enemy #104
Shining Hour #145

Silhouette Intimate Moments

Sweetheart Contract #4
Objections Overruled #53
Love Scene #100
Star Rise #116

PAT WALLACE

lives in New York's Greenwich Village with her husband, who is the inspiration for all her heroes. She is also devoted to their several cats and to her writing, which has been her very successful career for many years.

For my editor, Leslie J. Wainger,
and her patience, intelligence
and grace.

ACKNOWLEDGMENTS

Many thanks to the marvelous NASA and
Fodor publications,
and to Bill Anderson, as always.

Chapter 1

"What's this appointment about, Ma?" Charlie asked, excited. "Are you going to be the next woman in space?"

"Not so fast," Lisa Heron cautioned, grinning at her daughter's enthusiasm. "It's just a conference about a technical matter." Lisa studied Charlie with loving approval, glad the girl had gotten over her heavy makeup phase. Lisa sat under the big canvas umbrella, but Charlie's chair was in the late June sun; her blond hair glimmered in its light, her blue-gray eyes and rosy mouth gentle points of color against her tanned and flawless skin.

Not for the first time Lisa marveled that teenagers could come up with a name like "Charlie" for someone so feminine, then marveled even more that she'd chosen an old-fashioned name like Charlotte. Right now, though, Lisa was more preoccupied with her own evident calm; the two o'clock appointment with the space rep was something to get excited about.

Dr. Lisa Heron had qualified three years ago as a mission specialist, both in aeronautical engineering and space psychiatry, and was still awaiting assignment to a flight. Like others in the space program, she'd returned to her regular post on the staff of New York University in Manhattan's Greenwich Village. She taught, treated patients and engaged in research. Some of the research related to space—sleep and endurance studies, interviews with astronaut candidates in the area.

But all that was a long way from Houston and Cape Canaveral. And often, what with the budget cuts and decline in public interest, it seemed to Lisa that she was never going to get a flight. Then recently the first women had gone into space. Maybe, Lisa thought now, my time is coming.

"This man flew all the way from Houston to see you?" Charlie demanded.

"I doubt it." Lisa smiled at her daughter. "If I were getting a flight, they wouldn't notify me this way. I think I'm just a stop along his route. Don't forget, there are all kinds of space-related industries upstate, and on Long Island and in Connecticut."

Charlie raised her graceful brows. "Uh-huh," she commented dryly. "And with all those shrinks in San Antone and Houston and everywhere else, he's coming to see you because you're the worst."

Lisa chuckled. "Okay, okay, you made your point." It wasn't usual, of course, for a psychiatrist to have an engineering background, too. But the daughter of Philip Marley had not had the usual father. A Flying Tiger in World War II, Phil Marley had returned to civilian life on fire to conquer space. He'd joined the space program at its inception, working with Von Braun in Huntsville, and the family had moved all over, to Texas and Tennessee and Maryland, then to Cape Canaveral in Florida.

Lisa Heron had grown up with wind tunnels. A rocket gantry was as familiar to her as a swing. Then along the line she'd met Jack Heron and adopted New York as her home.

Silent now, Lisa gazed at Washington Square, across the street from the university's terrace restaurant where they were sitting. That was the only rub in a space assignment, she thought: leaving New York, which she loved so much. The terrace afforded a fine view of the busy square, the gathering-spot of Greenwich Village. Space flight seemed so unreal, considering the small-town air of their lives in this metropolis of millions. She and Charlie lived only blocks away from their respective office and school in a narrow house on West Twelfth Street.

On this brilliant summer day the park was attracting crowds of people. Lisa saw children on skateboards skim the man-made mounds at the center of the park; nearby a trim, middle-aged man was doing hand-over-hand exercises on the monkey bars, which reminded Lisa that she'd be forty in September. But she neither looked nor felt it. Part of staying qualified for a mission was keeping fit, and she'd done her time in the gym these last three years.

Her gaze wandered further. The usual chess players maneuvered their small ivory armies on the concrete tables at the MacDougal Street corner of the square. A group of tourists snapped pictures.

Charlie giggled. "Greg would freak if you got a flight. He's such a nerd about it."

The comical word always tickled Lisa. She chuckled in spite of herself. There was no getting around it. Charlie would always look on Greg Hamilton as a museum piece. He was one of the best neurologists in the East, gifted and civilized. Too civilized. He looked askance at Lisa's involvement in the space program. And if they ever married...

Suddenly Lisa wondered if she'd ever really wanted to. Damn it, she wasn't a kid...but she still felt entitled to be...well, carried away. Maybe she'd had a half-baked idea of giving Charlie a "proper father," having deprived her of her real one with the divorce. But that was nonsense. Charlie was a whole, healthy person who still had a perfectly good relationship with her father.

Now she saw four lean young black boys in the square. They wore apple-red T-shirts identifying them as "Option, a cappella Group." They started harmonizing in sweet, high tenors the sound of rainy wind. It was a lovely song, but it pinched Lisa with loneliness. She hadn't related to a love song for a long, long time.

"Ummm. And speaking of *love,*" Charlie said abruptly. She was staring at the flight of steps leading down to the terrace from the offices above.

Automatically Lisa *shush*ed her; Charlie's voice carried. Nevertheless, she was able to glimpse what Charlie was looking at. Or rather, whom.

A deeply tanned, muscular man was coming down the stairs, looking around for a table. Lisa hadn't seen many people like him since she'd trained in Houston and San Antonio. He reminded her a little of her father. Men like that were not a common sight in New York. He didn't look like a native. He was dressed in neat, casual civilian clothes, but his posture and the shortness of his light brown hair were somehow military. Her father had had a name for that look: the wild-blue-yonder syndrome.

Against the tanned face the newcomer's eyes blazed like blue neon. Lisa could feel that penetrating stare zoom in on her. The stare was bluer than the Capri grotto or a vivid October sky on a rare autumn morning; and gave the man's face a reckless, piratical look.

Disconcerted, Lisa glanced away. The incorrigible Charlie was studying her. But this time, to Lisa's relief, her daughter spoke in an undertone. "Now that's a *turn on*. If he wasn't so ancient, I'd be in love."

"Yes," Lisa retorted, "he's falling apart. He must be forty if he's an hour." She gave Charlie the eye.

Her daughter chortled. "Sorry about that." Covertly she examined the man again. "He's checking you out, Ma. I wonder what his sign is. A fire sign, I bet you ten dollars."

Charlie was a devotee of astrology, claiming that people with the "right" birth dates were "dynamite" together. Her triumph had been complete when Lisa told her that space personnel were required to take astronomy courses, memorize the zodiacal constellations and identify hundreds of navigational stars. Charlie and Lisa often engaged in a friendly, laughing debate about it. Charlie reminded her mother that the astrologers had been the first astronomers.

Once, to be fair about it, Lisa had read some of Charlie's astrology books. She'd been pleasantly astonished at their scholarly tone. One had been written by a prestigious woman whose family had included a U.S. president, the other by a British woman astrologer who sounded anything but misled. In fact, it had been downright spooky. The books had been right on target in evaluating Jack, Lisa's ex-husband, the status-seeking plastic surgeon whose sun sign of Capricorn was alleged to be so "difficult" for Lisa's sign of Libra.

All the same, Lisa had concluded that even if the great Jung had relied on astrology in his own work, she herself was still not convinced.

"I wonder if he's an Aries," Charlie ruminated. "That's what you need, Ma, to give your life pizzazz."

Lisa decided it was time to change the subject. "You never did tell me what your dad said on the phone." Lisa was eternally grateful for the fact that her daughter and her former husband were still in touch, and that Charlie also got along well with her stepmother.

"Oh, yes. Well, they invited me to stay with them up at the Cape this summer, after you and I have been to the island." Charlie and Lisa generally spent the month of July on Fire Island. "Bett"—Lisa was always a bit amused by the fancy abbreviation for Elizabeth—"said that we could go down to Boston and shop for some of my school things."

"Well, she could certainly help you with that," Lisa commented. Bett was a highly paid fashion coordinator. "Would you like to go?"

"I wouldn't mind," Charlie said casually.

"I have a feeling Rod's going to be there...right?" Lisa grinned. Charlie seemed to have a special feeling for Rod Benton, whose family had a summer cabin down the beach from Jack's.

"You're a witch," Charlie teased her, laughing. "So can I? Will you be too lonesome?"

"I think I'll manage," Lisa said dryly. "I *will* be working; the only psychiatrist in the world who's in town in August."

Charlie's giggle broke out again.

Mike Nesbitt sipped his iced coffee, eyeing the two beautiful women with blond hair. The younger one was as cute as she could be, but the older one—he guessed she was an older sister, because they looked so much alike—was a beauty. She looked as sharp as a needle, and she even had a sense of humor, because the kid kept laughing. Mike hadn't been able to hear what they were saying, but whatever the older one was saying had to be funny.

He gave her a discreet recon, starting at high altitude. She had gorgeous hair, smooth and lovely, like all the rest of her. None of this nutty look he'd noticed in Dallas and New York lately—the three-sizes-too-big gear, right out of *La Strada*, the hairdos that made the prettiest women look like they'd been blown out of a wind tunnel or dragged up from splashdown, dripping.

No, sir, this was a *woman*. Mike surmised she was in her late twenties. He checked out her face again: light tan; neat, classic features; small but sensuous mouth. Her eyes were big and brown and soft-looking, very intelligent. That combination of blond hair and dark eyes was something. It reminded Mike of what a character had said in some book he'd read, or some play he'd seen—"The ones with black eyes and yellow hair are hot as mustard."

A titillating idea. He shifted in his chair a little, his shirt feeling sticky on his back. Mike liked everything about that woman, even the way her black-and-tan dress hugged her body just enough. She wasn't wearing a wedding ring. Her only ornaments were a businesslike gold watch and a gold chain around her slender throat.

She had smashing legs.

He wished he could meet her. Well, there was no way to do that. You couldn't just start talking to that kind of woman.

Mike consulted his own heavy chronometer. It was almost time for his conference with the shrink, and he wanted to be aggressively early. He smiled to himself, remembering his confrontations with the mind-boys before his earlier flights. It had always been an in joke with the guys, fooling the shrinks as much as possible. Even now Mike Nesbitt had a certain nostalgia for the times he'd heard about, when men were more pilots than scientists and thought the psychological aspect was malarkey.

He signaled for his check, picturing the doctor he was scheduled to meet. Rayburn, who knew her, said she was a real gorgon. She certainly had an impressive record. Engineering and psychiatry were an uncommon blend even in a program full of versatile, bright people. Mike could just see her: one of those weathered types with the twinkly eyes that could turn to steel in a second. A female Heinz.

He nodded to the waiter and paid his bill, thinking, we didn't have enough trouble with nose cones and computers; now the mucky-mucks have got me in the psychiatry business. Well, maybe some sweet talk will help.

When he passed the brown-eyed beauty's table Mike gave her one last slow, covert look, determined to find out somehow who she was.

Lisa carefully ignored the blue-eyed man and looked at her watch. "Uh-oh. I'm cutting it pretty close. My appointment's at two, and I've got some things to do first."

"I hope it's about a flight." Charlie's blue-gray eyes were glowing.

Lisa smiled. "I'm afraid it won't be. So what are your plans?"

"First I'll call Dad. Then I'm going to meet Ruth. There's a Bogart festival at the Quint. We'll probably get some dinner after, okay? Anyway, I'll probably call you."

"Fine." Lisa paid the bill and stood up.

"Oh!" Charlie exclaimed. "I almost forgot." She slid a paperback book out of her canvas carryall and handed it to Lisa. "This is a really neat book, a kind of fantasy. The whole thing's based on astrology."

"I like the cover." Lisa glanced at it. "It should be fun to read. Thank you." She leaned to Charlie and kissed her soundly.

Charlie grinned. "You'll love the part about Aries and Libra. It starts right out with that." There was a mischievous sparkle in her eyes. "See you tonight, Ma."

She held up her hand and walked away to the street stairs. Lisa looked after her with fond eyes, then headed up the other set of stairs toward her office. She could use a twenty-seven-hour day, Lisa decided. The book looked so enjoyable that she'd have liked to start reading it right then. Some hope. After the conference with the spaceman she had three patients scheduled.

What's more, her brief talk with Charlie about a flight had fired her again with an idea she'd been working on, the notion of psychological research on weightlessness. What would its effect be on the human brain, the psyche? Other psychiatrists she'd talked to had been lukewarm about the project, claiming there wouldn't be enough "interest." Maybe younger psychiatrists would have greater enthusiasm....

Lisa was so preoccupied that she found herself in her office almost before she knew it. The office had a separate waiting room with a closed door. Lisa liked the idea of screening visitors and sensitive patients from the impersonal office business and giving them quiet and privacy, so as usual she asked her secretary Jan, "Anyone?"

"The flyboy's here early," Jan answered impassively. Observing her secretary's bland, almost bored expression, Lisa wondered for the hundredth time what had possessed Jan to take this job. She would have been a perfect receptionist for Lisa's ex-husband, the fashionable plastic surgeon. As a matter of fact, Charlie had said that both Jan and Jack were the same astrological sign, Capricorn. Lisa wondered why that had occurred to her.

Most likely it stemmed from the conversation with Charlie and her daughter's insistence that Lisa "needed an Aries." Also because of the book Charlie had given her. Well, she'd better get her mind on the two o'clock appointment. She thanked Jan, adding, "Okay. Buzz me at two." Jan nodded her sleek auburn head once and immediately returned to her typing.

Lisa closed her door, sat down at her desk and opened the space folder again, reluctantly putting Charlie's book aside. What was the officer's name again? She consulted his letter. Nesbitt. Lieutenant Colonel Michael Nesbitt. She'd tuned in to a tone of veiled skepticism in Nesbitt's letter when he referred to "alleged" psychological problems among his team. Her respected old friend, Dr. Dieter Heinz, had evaluated them and expressed a cautious and tentative agreement. Lisa thought of the wise-guy astronauts she'd met. Nesbitt had already flown five missions, but she'd never met him. With that rank he must be one of the older ones, she thought, and she could just picture him—the hard-bitten warrior type, like that general in the movie who thought that a woman's place was in the garden, with a flower in her hair.

Just for the hell of it, she decided to look him up in one of her space-program publications. There was no picture of him, oddly enough, but his birth date was listed as April 4, in the same year as her own. An Aries. He had been born in Florida. Lisa recalled something Charlie had said about Aries men, that they were an odd combination of conservatism and daring. Well, that certainly fit her idea of Lt. Col. Michael Nesbitt.

I must be cracking up, Lisa accused herself. What on earth did the man's *persona* matter, except as it might affect her work, her professional position? Lisa wondered what was happening to her. Maybe it had all begun with that beautiful love song the boys had been singing in the square, something about love being just a memory.

And then that man coming down the stairs, the man with the eyes like blue fire. He'd had an air of utter confidence and power, very different from her own swaying "Libra temperament," as Charlie called it, claiming that her mother balanced everything on her scales.

Lisa shook her head and forced her attention back to the folder.

The buzzer startled her.

Hastily Lisa examined her face and hair in her compact mirror, checking for neatness, then depressed the intercom button and said, "Please send Colonel Nesbitt in."

She got up and walked toward the opening door.

The man from the terrace, the man with the blazing blue eyes, was standing on the threshold. His expression of amazement was almost comical.

Lisa's first wild impulse was to laugh. She controlled herself with an effort.

Then, as their gazes held, the situation stopped being funny anymore. She was overcome with a peculiar sensation of chilliness in the pit of her stomach and she thought, oh, no. No. This *can't* be Nesbitt.

She got hold of herself and said calmly, "Please, Colonel Nesbitt. Sit down." She gestured toward the dark brown leather chair before her desk.

He was still staring at her. Then he seemed to come awake, too, and murmured, "Thank you." But he was still standing, obviously waiting for her to sit down. The Southern gentleman, she reflected, half approving, half irritated. His emphasis on her sex somehow put the interview on a less than professional basis.

All of a sudden his white grin slashed his tanned face, and he drawled, "I thought you'd make me lie down on your couch."

This was the first time she'd heard his voice at full force, and she was positively dismayed at the effect. It was very strong without being especially deep, and for some reason it reminded her of a chorus of brasses she'd heard one afternoon from the tower of the nearby Judson Church. She felt that strange chill again.

Yet *what* he'd said, and his mocking expression, angered her. It was as if he thought the whole psychiatric profession were one big joke.

"If you need the couch, feel free," she retorted coolly. She raised her brows and gestured at the brown leather couch by the wall, but as soon as the words were out of her mouth she regretted them. That was a comment that could be taken quite another way, she decided.

To her annoyance he picked up on it right away. "If I admit to that, I might hang myself in two ways, Doctor." He grinned wickedly.

This whole thing was getting off course, she thought, and, ignoring his last comment, asked if he'd like some coffee.

"No, thanks. I had some already, out on the terrace...where you were sitting with your sister."

My sister, she echoed in disgusted silence. She passed over the crude flattery and sat down at her desk. She took her owlish reading glasses from a holder and put them on, then skimmed his letter to gain some time. He was sitting now, very tall in the big chair, staring at her. For some reason that sent her into a tailspin.

She had to get them back to business. "I take it that this investigation is primarily your idea, Colonel."

Nesbitt smiled lopsidedly. "You take it right. In spite of Heinz's tentative conclusions, Rayburn and his engineers seem to think the pogo's in my men...and me. I've flown enough missions to have a gut feeling when something's not right with the hardware. And intuitive fear in this case is hardly abnormal; it's only good horse sense. I don't have to tell you we're in the business of imponderables twenty-six hours a day." His grin widened. "I'm not putting anybody down. I happen to think that your background uniquely suits you to head an investigation. So does Heinz."

Lisa warmed at that, thinking of Dieter Heinz. Nesbitt's arguments sounded reasonable, but he was still a bit high-handed for an astronaut-engineer, no matter how prestigious his job was...setting himself up as an expert on normality.

"What do you think? I imagine you've had some time to study the reports," Nesbitt prodded.

She hesitated so long that he said, "Doctor...?"

"Oh, yes," she said. Now she was getting to him, she could see. He probably thought he'd have to pull conclusions out of her with a pair of pliers. And she wondered, too, why she was acting like this; she never did. Why did he seemed to rub her the wrong way?

"And...?" he prompted again, revealing some impatience.

"The pogo you mentioned, Colonel..." That was a very familiar word to her, from childhood. "Pogo" was astronaut slang for a mysterious vibration that could rarely be traced or fixed, that often simply disappeared all by itself. "I take it you experienced it personally?"

He raised his brows. "Tell me, Doctor, why is it that shrinks always answer a question with a question?"

She started laughing. She noticed that his look dropped to her mouth, that he began to answer her laughter with a broad grin. "Touché," she conceded. "But did you?"

"Yes, I did. I'm here to tell you I never heard anything so weird in my life. And, I might add, it's nice not to have to remind a doctor what pogo is." He was still smiling and their gazes touched.

"I'm Phil Marley's daughter," she said.

"Phil *Marley*?" His expression was one of awe. People always reacted like that to her father's name. "The grand old man...the pioneer. How is he? *Where* is he? Why isn't he still in the program?" The questions tumbled out.

Nesbitt's expression was so earnest, he was so sincerely interested, that Lisa couldn't be offended by his quiz. But he flushed. "I'm sorry. I'm being awfully personal. But you see, he's always been one of my heroes, since I was a kid."

Lisa wanted to tell him the truth, all of a sudden. But she couldn't, because of the promise to her father. So she said simply, "He's been very ill. He's been living a very secluded and inactive life."

"I'm sorry, *really* sorry." The vivid eyes were curious, but at the same time compassionate. Lisa felt much warmer toward him. At the same time, in just these few minutes the conference had taken off in an informal, friendly direction, and she felt a bit out of control.

"Apparently, then," she resumed briskly, "you have a serious technical problem, and you think your men's reactions are highly unusual."

"Unusual's not the word. You've studied their backgrounds. It doesn't make sense. And then consider Heinz's opinion."

True. She respected her old friend Dieter Heinz more than almost anyone. His conclusion, though cautious, meant something.

"Come to Houston," Nesbitt said eagerly. "Handle it for us."

"Just like *that,* Colonel? If it were a *flight,* it would be a different matter. As it is, I've got a practice, research plans, family obligations...."

"Obligations to your sister?"

Here it was again, the personal prodding. She wished she'd never told him who her father was.

"She's my daughter, Colonel Nesbitt."

"Your *daughter?"* His surprise was so real that she couldn't help being pleased, even though this wasn't the first time she'd heard that. "Well, I'll be damned." Then he asked with elaborate casualness, "Would your husband's wishes enter in?"

"Hardly," she said dryly. "I've been divorced five years." It irritated and amused her that he'd gotten so much personal information out of her. She was used to being the sounding board, encouraging people to open up to her. And she noticed something else, an unmistakable look of elation in his cobalt-blue eyes.

"I *see.*"

Damnation, those eyes went right through her, making her feel untouched and new. A forty-year-old divorcée with a college-age daughter, feeling untouched.

He was probably all too aware of his effect on women, she thought. This was exactly why he'd come for a personal interview. Well, she wasn't going to let him maneuver her into a hasty decision.

She leaned back in her chair, observing him through her big glasses. "There's a great deal involved in my leaving New York," she said.

"If it's a money matter..." he began, but she shook her head, "or...whatever, I have carte blanche to help you arrange things. We'll put you up in the best hotel, fly you in a VIP jet...if you can just come down for a few days, look the situation over, set up procedures."

"Colonel, it wouldn't be a matter of *days*. There's no predicting how long this could take."

"So much the better," he remarked with a grin. "It'll be a pleasure to work with you, Doctor. Besides, if you happened to get a flight, you'd be right there to begin your retraining."

"You can get me a flight?" she asked impulsively, excited. Then she realized she'd fallen right into his trap. It was blackmail, no more, no less. If he had that much clout...

"I'd be lying if I gave you a guarantee, but I'd do my damnedest. And I know the agency would count it in your favor."

"I appreciate your frankness," she said. It sounded chancy. But already she was debating with herself, asking, why not? Maybe Charlie's summer schedule could be rearranged. There was only one research project, and that could wait. Her patients could be transferred to another therapist.

When Lisa looked up at him again, she caught a triumphant expression on Nesbitt's face and wavered. She had a feeling she'd been talked into something. But she wanted a flight so *much*.

"I can't give you an answer right now, Colonel." She saw his face fall.

"We need to know soon, Dr. Heron," he said quietly.

"How soon?"

"Yesterday," he retorted with that impudent grin. More seriously he added, "Tomorrow...or the next day?"

Tomorrow. "I'll have to think about it. Where can I reach you?" She offered him a memo pad and pen. He scribbled on the pad, tore off the sheet and handed it to her.

"That's my hotel. Leave a message there anytime. And meanwhile I'll stay in touch with you." He looked at her meaningfully, and she gave him one of her cards.

"Please, Doctor, think about it hard. It's vital to us to have you in on this thing."

He was using all his powerful appeal, and it raised new doubts in her, new suspicions. She began to wonder if the half promise of a flight was an outright bribe, if he'd expect her to come up with the "right" conclusions in return. People had tried that with her before. She was going to have to give this a whole lot of thought, find out everything she could about his background before she decided.

"I'll let you know," she said. Then she glanced at her watch. "You'll have to forgive me now. I have a patient scheduled soon." Lisa got up, taking off her glasses.

He got up, too, but to her annoyance said in an almost intimate tone, "That's so much better."

"I beg your pardon?"

"Without the glasses. It's a crime to hide eyes like yours...Doctor."

He was impossible, she decided.

"I'll be waiting, Dr. Heron." He held out his hand and she took it. It almost swallowed hers, and the rasp of his calloused palm, the heated pressure of his strong fingers, had an astonishing result.

The man's sexual magnetism was awesome. It took all her poise not to wince. Slowly she withdrew her hand from his.

Nesbitt looked down at their hands, then raised his head to look again into her eyes. More than ever, his own eyes struck her like blue fire.

She realized with dismay that she was actually dizzy.

With another significant look at her, he strode out, closing the door gently.

Lisa sank down in her chair with an explosive sigh. No wonder she was dizzy. She reassured herself that it wasn't just a strong reaction to an attractive man; it was the whole sudden proposal, his casual suggestion that she rearrange her entire life overnight.

She smiled at herself. She supposed she was pretty hide-bound, a little stuffy for an astronaut. But that was a whole other issue: assignment to flight followed an orderly, cut-and-dried procedure, with months allowed for psychological and other adjustments. But *this*...If he had his way, she'd be in Houston tomorrow...or tonight.

Charlie would love this, she thought wryly; he's a textbook Aries, according to her way of thinking, rushing right into a project, only to abandon it. Maybe he'd abandon *her*, forget his blithe promise to get her a flight. She had to find out more about him; the astronaut roster listed only objective data.

Lisa checked her watch again. She still had a few minutes before Mrs. Prentice came. She dialed a friend at Montefiore Hospital, with whom she'd worked on a sleep study years ago, and asked if she could find a psychological profile of Nesbitt. "If we don't have one here," the friend said, "I know just where to get it. Shall I mail it to you?"

"Phone me, if you would." Lisa tried her best to sound casual. "I want to work on something this weekend."

"Will do," her contact said, sounding blessedly incurious.

Lisa was in no mood for Mrs. Prentice. She had too much on her mind—this upheaval and, she admitted, Michael Nesbitt. She hadn't experienced anything like that thunderclap of feeling for nearly twenty years. Just from the touch of the man's fingers, too. That brief contact had been so...intimate.

Then she concluded that even Mrs. Prentice would be a relief from this brooding. So when Jan buzzed her, telling her that the woman had arrived, she was more receptive.

Mrs. Prentice always strained her patience. Even though she wasn't supposed to like or dislike a patient, Lisa had to concede that she didn't like this one.

During the session she had a hard time being objective about the woman's complaints, the whining conclusion that her son was abandoning her by choosing an out-of-state rather than a local college.

The fact that his special interests could be met only at the distant school cut no ice, much as Lisa tried to help Mrs. Prentice see it. The truth was that the woman had submerged herself so completely in her son that she had no life of her own, hardly a self of her own. At one point Lisa had to bite her tongue to keep from saying, "You should try being a single mother."

At the end of the session, while Lisa was taking a breather before the next patient came in, the phone buzzed. It was her Montefiore colleague, who gave her a skillfully capsuled version of the profile of Michael Nesbitt. Lisa pretended to be writing it down and listened breathlessly.

The subject showed exceptional courage and daring, the report said, and, while seemingly open, had a number of "secret places." According to the report it would take "a psychiatric Sherlock Holmes" to unravel him. While he was compassionate and kind with no overt hostility, he could be "ruthless, a Machiavelli" in his approach to attaining his ends.

He was sexually healthy and normal, but had a strong aversion to permanent commitment.

Lisa thanked her colleague and hung up. So this was the hidden side of Michael Nesbitt. She had suspected as much. If he were that Machiavellian, feeling that the end justified the means, he could easily be manipulating her with that promise of a flight.

The idea was still haunting her when her next patient arrived. His session, and the one after, were draining. By a quarter to six she felt exhausted. Dinner with Greg would be impossible. She caught him just before he left his office, pleading tiredness. His disappointment was plain, but he treated her with his usual consideration.

That very quality perversely annoyed Lisa. He seemed so namby-pamby, so damned correct. Another kind of man might offer to bring Chinese food to her office, tell her to put her feet up while he rubbed her neck. A man like...Nesbitt?

Lisa twitted herself; she was just a little nutty from pressure. After Jan left she massaged the back of her neck for herself.

The bright cover of Charlie's book caught her attention. That would be just the way to unwind. The school offices were open until nine, so she could stay right here and enjoy the novel at her leisure.

Lisa picked up the book and opened it to the title page—*The House of Stars.* That had a pleasant, almost fairy-tale sound. The author's name was unfamiliar. The next page was titled, "Part I, The Horns of Fire," below that, *Aries-Libra.* Titillated, Lisa went on to the first chapter. Soon she realized she'd gobbled up the first hundred pages in utter absorption.

She put the open book face down, reflecting that the writer had an extraordinary imagination. Lisa had recognized many star names from her NASA classes. The author had used them for character names.

Lisa gathered that the section she'd read was the first of a series of love stories involving the astrological "opposites," which were allegedly quite magnetic. The whole thing was delightful because it reminded her so much of astronomy, a subject she was passionately interested in. Furthermore, it seemed to confirm a great many things Charlie had said about her own favorite subject, astrology.

"Aries-Libra," Lisa murmured.

Michael Nesbitt was an Aries; she herself was a Libra.

Feeling a bit juvenile, but unable to resist the impulse, Lisa reread the description of the book's Aries hero: *His voice was hard and brilliant, like the trumpets; his eyes were bright as turquoise in his long, tanned Arien face.*

Lisa pictured Nesbitt. His voice reminded her again of the concert of brasses she'd heard played from the Judson Tower.

She noticed the author's frequent use of the word "brazen," a musical, rather dated word Lisa liked. It meant "bold" as well as suggesting the sound and color of brass instruments. Nesbitt was certainly brazen, in more ways than one, she thought wryly.

But this was absolutely absurd. It was one thing to be charmed by a book, by someone's lyrical imagination, quite another to make a hero of a manipulative flyboy she'd met only a couple of hours ago.

"I need a shrink myself," she said aloud. Uneasily, however, she recalled that the novel's hero was also a daredevil pilot, a native of the country "Fiamma"—Italian for "flame"—the country of the "fire people," which strongly suggested Florida, where Nesbitt came from, and Houston, Texas, capital of space.

The Libra heroine came from a metropolis in the East, from the "air country." The parallel was eerie.

Then her sense of proportion was restored. The plain fact was that her metabolism was out of whack from simple hunger. As a doctor she was well aware that lack of food could make the mind play tricks. It was such a relief that she laughed. She was going to get right out of here, have dinner in a nice place, and then go home and watch TV, putting off a decision about Houston until later.

With the book in her handbag, Lisa left the building. Then she began to stroll through Washington Square. Because of daylight saving time, it was still light, but the temperature had undergone a rapid change. There was now the slightest coolness in the wind, and Lisa felt more comfortable in her clothes, glad of the slight weight of the raw silk coat that matched her dress.

All of a sudden everything felt just right, her clothes, her work, her child—all the rest of her life—or most of it, she amended, thinking of her father.

Whenever she thought of his current situation, she ached. First there had been that horrible accident that had caused the death of the three astronauts, with her father, despite every disclaimer, taking the blame. Then the deepening depression, so paralyzing that he could no longer function. And after that, the secrecy about the matter, and her father's plea that it be kept quiet.

He'd always had a horror of mental disturbances, the distaste of a healthy, strong, adventurous man for illness of that kind in himself. And it had been her father's illness that had first led Lisa into medicine, then into psychiatry, caused her to abandon her idea of becoming an engineer. But during the last year her father had been steadily improving, and she wanted to be here when he was released.

There was so much to hold her in New York, she thought. She sat down on a bench, still reflecting. A career she loved, her daughter, a beautiful house in the city that had become her heart's home.

As to the colonel and his all-fired charm—he was only another manipulator who thought a lot of himself. It might be fun to fly to Houston for a few days, to see what was going on, but she couldn't make a longer commitment. If they wanted her for a flight, let them notify her through the regular channels.

Dealing with Nesbitt was no longer a challenge. She already knew some of the things that made him tick. As for that electricity between them, that was simple enough. She was a perfectly healthy woman who'd been too damned fastidious for too damned long.

The conclusion buoyed her, and she got up from the bench, walking on under the Washington arch, where she good-naturedly dodged a sweating girl on a bicycle.

Then she caught the mournful sound of mandolins. She glanced west. An old man and his brothers, familiar neighborhood characters, were serenading the passersby at their regular hour. They always drew a crowd because their playing was spirited, poignant and full of simple emotion.

The strings plucked at Lisa's heart. The light was dying around her, and she realized how brief the dusk was in Manhattan in the summer. For a moment there was that fine hyacinth color, the heliotrope of twilight when all the air turned azure, like the "blue hour" in Paris. Then, zap! The dark.

The mandolins trilled the grand old tearjerker "Sorrento," and suddenly it was as moving as an operatic aria. Lisa recalled the mythical country of Fiamma.

She suddenly experienced a hunger pang in the midst of all her romantic notions.

She quickened her pace and walked toward Greene Street, where she'd have a choice of several pleasant restaurants. On Greene itself was the cozy Givus à Quiche. Despite its cutesy name she liked its light dinners. But she needed something more substantial after a day like this. At the corner of Waverly and Greene was the beautiful Thai place, Bells of Siam, with its golden dragons and flamboyant eaves, brass bells and ceremonial cloths. Never mind brass bells; she'd had enough brass for one day.

Lisa opted for her favorite, Harbin's. Outside it were small trees in urns, their branches decorated with tiny white lights in a cool, perpetual silver Christmas. Through the filmy drapes she glimpsed pale pink napery and gentle lights, glimmering votive candles on each table in fluted, tulip-shaped crystal holders. It looked very inviting.

When she went in, the maître d', Georges, greeted her warmly. "How many this evening?" She'd come here often with Greg, with Charlie and her colleagues.

"Only me tonight." She smiled.

"There's nothing 'only' about you, Dr. Heron," Georges said gallantly. He led her to a small table near the window. She ordered a cocktail, feeling herself relax, and looked around the lovely room: nothing but couples. She felt extremely solo.

She decided to reread something that had caught her fancy in the book.

There it was, the one particular line that had stuck in her memory: *She stared into the turquoise eyes of Hamal, the incorrigible Arien whose sun sign was in fatal opposition to her own.*

Fatal opposition...a fascinating, loaded phrase.

Lisa looked up, savoring the expression. A man was standing outside Harbin's window, looking in.

It was Michael Nesbitt.

Chapter 2

He gave Lisa a wide smile and held up his hand in salute. Against the background of the fragile trees strung with their small white lights he looked even more rugged and imposing than usual.

She smiled uncertainly in return and was struck with a lovely, vagrant thought: the tiny white lights reminded her of a miniature galaxy of mysterious planets and stars. For that one instant Nesbitt was standing in unexplored space. Lisa questioned her own fanciful reaction. This man had an astonishing effect, if seeing him could make her think like this. It was probably the result of reading that unusual book. Nesbitt was the last person in the world she needed right now.

And he was coming into the restaurant. She saw him head for the entrance.

When he came into view she noticed that he'd changed clothes. He was wearing a midnight-blue lightweight suit, the shade of the late evening sky, and a pale blue shirt. His dark blue tie with a jagged pattern of cobalt blue reminded her of lightning. Appropriate, because this encounter was suddenly a hundred times more jarring than her first sight of him on the terrace. Those vivid eyes of his seemed to burn in the gentle light, and Lisa felt a disconcerting tremor in her knees that spread to her whole body.

Nesbitt murmured, smiling and urbane, to the impressed Georges, who practically beamed, then headed toward Lisa's table. Even with the new smoothness of his appearance, he looked bigger and more reckless than before. He seemed to mock the pastel elegance surrounding them, to diminish the very proportions of the room.

Trying to compose herself, Lisa decided, I can't ever work with this man. Then, he was standing by the table.

"May I join you for a minute, Dr. Heron?"

For the first time it occurred to her that his brows were V-shaped, with a hornlike effect...like the man in that book. Lisa's imaginative reflections surprised her. Now *she* was experiencing a pogo. But she was determined not to let him know it.

"Am I already under surveillance?" she asked lightly.

Once again he turned her quip around and answered in a soft tone, "You have been since one-thirty this afternoon. And you're still answering a question with a question, Doctor."

"But you didn't answer it fully, Colonel." However, she gestured for him to sit down. It seemed very rude to keep him standing there. Besides, they were attracting attention, something that she always found distasteful. "Is this the agency's way of checking me out?"

He admired her with his eyes, ignoring the last question. "Thank you for letting me join you like this." He said it without irony, sounding as if she'd granted him an enormous favor. "I see we're both late diners," he added, smiling again.

Lisa had the feeling that he took that social tone for several reasons—one was to give her time to compose herself, to get used to his presence. She decided that he must be psychic to know she needed that. Another reason was that he seemed to be nervous himself. That touched her in spite of herself, reassured her somehow. She was suddenly slightly ashamed of digging into his background like a spy. She said more warmly, "I just left my office. I...didn't expect to see you again so soon. Are you staying in the area?"

Nesbitt stared at her intently. "Yes. Right around the corner, as a matter of fact, at Fifth and Tenth. I've been AWOL this afternoon, wandering around the Village."

"It's a good place to wander. There's a lot to see."

There was a brief silence, then he asked, "Do you always work this late?"

Lisa shook her head. The waiter brought him a cocktail and took his dinner order. After the man had gone, she said, "Not usually."

Nesbitt took a sip of his drink and his gaze brushed the book beside her plate. "I interrupted your reading. Is that an astronomy book?"

"Indirectly." She smiled. "It's a novel, a fantasy based on astrology...the old-time astronomy."

"Well, well." He grinned widely. "My mother practically raised me on that. I've never seen any fiction based on it before. May I?"

She handed him the book, noting that he was careful to keep a finger in her place while he riffled through the pages. "Aha. Good old Hamal. My astronomy prof in San Antone said it was a very hard star to find. Would you believe my mother almost *named* me that? Can you picture 'Hamal Nesbitt'?"

She chuckled. "Not easily." She was feeling very friendly toward him now, warming to their common interest.

"Aries and Libra," he commented, quoting from the book, "the 'fatal opposites.'"

His eyes met hers. "You wouldn't be a Libra, by any chance?"

She couldn't help the flush that rose to her face. "I am, as a matter of fact." It was a relief when the waiter interrupted them to set Nesbitt's dinner before him.

He handed the book back to her, and when she took it their fingers met briefly. The effect of that swift contact was positively startling. A poignant dart of excitement pierced her fingertips, racing up her arm like a small shooting star.

Nesbitt was staring at her again, ignoring his food. "Zubeneschamali, the Libra star. The only one harder to find than Hamal."

The air between them was charged, like the electric feeling of the air before a storm. To lighten the weight of oppressive tension Lisa said, "As hard to say as it is to find. My daughter says it sounds like some exotic foreign dish."

Nesbitt chuckled. "That's very clever. It's obvious where she got her imagination." He began to eat his food with utter indifference, as if it were no more interesting than a slice of pizza.

"Why do you say that?" she parried.

"It's not every woman who wants to go into space...especially a woman like you."

The implied flattery was plain, and she couldn't help reacting to it with pride. She'd always taken care to preserve her total femininity while living up to every demand of both her training as an astronaut and her profession.

This whole encounter seemed to be the most natural thing in the world. But he'd charmed her into thinking that. This man was absolutely dangerous. No wonder he was in public relations. Before I know what's hit me, she reflected, I'll be packing for Houston, setting up a program for him, maybe even reaching his own foregone conclusions. Then waiting another three years, or five, or six, for a flight, the way those other women did.

Suddenly she felt less warm toward him, a little less relaxed.

"Colonel Nesbitt, please tell me why you're here...how you knew where I was."

He looked positively caught out. He put down his fork and pushed his plate away, abandoning dinner. "The simple truth is that I was waiting in Washington Square for you to come out of your office. I followed you." There was an abashed expression in his eyes, and a faint smile twitched at the corners of his mouth. "I wanted to see you. You've been on my mind since the minute I saw you on that terrace this afternoon. I couldn't believe you were the one I had the appointment with...you're so...." He stopped, reddening.

"What did you expect?" Lisa demanded, amusement and exasperation struggling with another feeling, something warm, foreign and expectant.

He laughed. "A kind of bearded lady, I guess."

The thought was so absurd that the corners of *her* mouth began to twitch.

It's getting worse and worse, she decided. How could she keep up a front when someone affected her the way Nesbitt did? But she wanted to bring her guard up again. "You haven't asked me about Houston."

That had been a mistake, because he said soberly, "No. I'm not working now, Lisa Heron."

His use of both her names sounded paradoxically personal. He could turn anything she said to his advantage. All her years of thrust-and-parry were failing her. Suddenly she thought of the fight-flight syndrome: some creatures turned and fought when threatened, others fled. Maybe she'd opt for flight. Appropriate enough in this case, she reflected with dry amusement.

"Well, this has been very pleasant," she said slowly, "but I'm afraid I'd better run along. My daughter's probably waiting for me at home." It occurred to her that Charlie hadn't called, although she'd only half promised to, but that really did bother her a bit. She got out her credit card, gesturing to Georges. She marked her place in the book and put it in her bag.

Nesbitt had frowned a little when she pulled out the credit card. She realized it was probably inconceivable to him that an escorted woman would act like that; he was still a Southerner, born and bred, it seemed, no matter how worldly he'd become. When the waiter came Nesbitt ignored Lisa's card and paid the bill in cash, murmuring, "I don't have the patience for all that plastic rigmarole," which Lisa found very typical.

"I'm sorry you have to go," he said softly. "I'll see you home, at least."

"Oh, no," Lisa protested quickly. "I'm only a few blocks away." She felt absurdly flurried.

"Where?"

"Twelfth Street," she answered, with a sense of being pressed, "between Fifth and Sixth."

"It's right on my way," he insisted, and it seemed silly to argue about it. They strolled along Waverly Place to Fifth Avenue, and when they turned the corner and started walking uptown it seemed to her that the familiar vista, with its red and green and amber traffic lights, its silvery lamps, had never looked so beautiful. The lights were enormous jewels this evening, the avenue the road to Oz, even if it wasn't paved with yellow bricks but with dark, pedestrian asphalt.

She was surprised but strangely exultant that everything seemed so new and strange. Apparently Michael Nesbitt had been thinking such things, too, because he said, "This is a wonderful city. I love it when they put the big Christmas tree under the Washington arch."

They were passing the romantic, dim-lit Washington Mews when he made the remark. She smiled at his almost boyish expression and then glanced into the small, sequestered mews. The converted carriage houses, which had once served as coach houses and stables for the big mansions on Washington Square North, were now luxury apartments behind a locked, grillwork gate. The light of the old-fashioned lanterns was gentle and mellow.

He followed her glance. "I always expect to see Rudolph and Mimi in there," he commented, grinning.

"You know, so do I," she admitted, feeling very warm toward him again. The reference to the characters from *La Bohème* seemed uncharacteristic at first, but then she realized that that was foolish; after all, the man was a colonel, and that rank implied a broadness of experience. Still, he was a complex character, more thoughtful than many of the other NASA pilots she'd run into, even the administrative ones like Nesbitt.

They crossed Eighth Street and wandered past the glass-enclosed restaurant at the corner, with its outdoor tables. The place was famous for its pianists, and now the faint strains of the rippling keys reached Lisa. It was a haunting Cole Porter tune.

"Nice," he said. "You know, this afternoon when I was on French leave, I saw the damnedest thing. A fellow was displaying a huge painting back there, on Fifth just past the square. It was his impression of the Sixties...a great big murallike affair. I looked at the thing for quite a while. Everything seemed to be there—the war, the flower children, John Kennedy and Martin Luther King. But you know, he'd left out the biggest thing of all. There wasn't a sign of the moon walk in sixty-nine. Can you imagine?" he demanded. "What kind of a way to think is that?"

"Outrageous," she agreed, meaning it. "The most exciting thing to come along in...history, and you mean he left it *out*?"

"That's what he did. I swear I couldn't believe it." Nesbitt put his hand under her elbow as they crossed Ninth Street.

"I can't either. I really can't. But somehow it's typical of the way things have been going in recent years...this utter lack of public interest in space." She was beginning to feel more and more related to him and the way he thought. Besides, the brief touch of his hand had had an amazing effect. Her whole arm tingled.

"It's going to change," he said with exuberant certainty. "Believe me, these manned shuttles are going to put us back on the map again...and back in the media." She glanced at him. He was smiling broadly.

They were silent the rest of the way. Lisa was glad, because she was busy coping with the odd new turmoil inside her. Michael Nesbitt was the most exciting man she'd met in years. And their minds appeared to mesh so utterly. But she reminded herself that she'd known him less than a day, that she'd made another mistake like this about Jack Heron. She'd let her ex-husband sweep her off into a lightning marriage, and then she'd found out what he was like at her remorseful leisure.

So when they turned onto Twelfth Street, passing the New School, Lisa felt her guard go up again.

"Which is your house?" he asked.

"Farther on," she said, "On the other side." Her voice sounded breathless and uncertain in her own ears, and she was aware of his close, warm scrutiny.

"Just over there," she directed, when they were closer. He took her arm in a protective gesture while they waited for two cars to pass, and then they crossed close together. She had very ambivalent feelings about his nearness. On the one hand, it was lovely, exciting. On the other, she knew that it was also highly dangerous.

"Pretty," he drawled, looking at the house. It was a slender red brick house only about two big windows wide, with a low stoop. The white door with its polished knocker was flanked by heavy pots of vivid begonias.

"I love it," she admitted, feeling her breath quicken. She had the sense that this was going to be a strategic and sticky moment, this time for saying goodnight.

Nesbitt wasn't making it any easier. He continued to stand there, staring down at her, and he looked more appealing than ever. The pale blue of his shirt collar made his coppery skin seem much darker in contrast; even in the navy-blue jacket, which would have diminished a less muscular man, his shoulders were immensely broad and strong. He smiled.

Amazingly Lisa recalled a line from the book she'd read: *His teeth were white as milk glass against the dark tan of his face.* When a car passed, its headlights reflected for an instant in Nesbitt's vivid eyes, she remembered also the descriptions of the man with "turquoise eyes."

She couldn't understand what was happening to her; she felt like a lovesick adolescent. This had to stop.

Lisa started to go in.

"Please," he said softly, "don't go in just yet...." She paused a split second. Encouraged, he repeated, "Please..." and then added, "Lisa."

The sound of her first name, spoken like that in his gentle but commanding voice, did something to her. All of a sudden she felt incapable of moving at all.

Before she was aware of it, she was in his arms. He was pulling her close with coaxing strength, and his hot, trembling mouth was exploring her brow, her cheekbone, the corner of her parted mouth.

With a big, shaky hand he turned her face toward his, and they discovered each other's mouths. Lisa felt her own mouth turn willing and soft; now her hunger to feel his lips was every bit as deep and aching as his own seemed. She found herself returning his caress with savage fervor. It seemed to her that all the loneliness of recent years, all her deprivation, was centered on the small flame of her mouth. She was shattered by the unexpected power of that kiss, bemused into a sudden, instantaneous submission. In those unmeasured seconds she was filled with an enormous sense of the inescapable.

Another car went by slowly, and she realized all at once exactly what they were doing, and where. Dr. Lisa Heron was kissing a comparative stranger on a public street, in front of her own house. Her own child might be watching.

In eerie counterpoint, when Lisa pulled away from Nesbitt, she saw her neighbor enter his house across the street. A burning wave of chagrin washed over her, and she heard herself murmur, "No, no," while he tried to draw her into his arms again. She heard his pained, breathy whisper, "Please, Lisa..."

She pulled away and rushed up the stoop to the narrow front door, and let herself in without looking back, thinking, I can't let this happen. I don't even know this man, and I trust him even less. She still couldn't believe that she had let that happen, that idiotic incident. She absolutely would not give up control like this, no matter how much her obstinate body demanded it.

Charlie was home. Lisa heard the soft rock that she favored drifting from the speakers in her daughter's room.

Lisa let out a great sigh, automatically replacing her keys in her bag, and put the bag on a table in the hall. She slipped off her silk coat and hung it in a closet.

"Ma? Hi!" Lisa looked up and saw her daughter leaning over the banister, grinning. Charlie's long golden hair almost hid her pretty face. All Lisa could see were her lips, her pert nose and the inner corners of her eyes. "Where've you been all this time? Not *working*?"

"Not all the time," Lisa said evasively. She felt a rush of mixed emotions—sheer relief that Charlie obviously hadn't seen what had been going on; sharp guilt, because she should be thinking about her daughter, not herself; and also, among other things, a tender new affection.

"Want me to fix you something?" Charlie called out as she rounded the banister and came running down the stairs. "You look a little wasted." Charlie was wearing one of her favorite things, a huge thrift-shop shirt that was as long on her as a mini, and she looked utterly charming, as usual.

But the comment about her own looks made Lisa turn nervously to the console mirror to check herself out. Good heavens, what if her lipstick were smeared, her hair all...However, a glance reassured her. She wore so little makeup that the passionate encounter with Nesbitt had left no sign. Besides, her fine, almost straight hair rarely got mussed. Nevertheless it seemed to Lisa that her eyes were bigger, more glowing than usual, and that her color was high.

"Ma...? Are you okay?" Charlie inquired, staring at her.

"Of course." Lisa started into the living room.

Charlie, following, remarked, "I thought I heard you talking to somebody outside. Who was it?"

Lisa hesitated a beat. Then she said as casually as she could manage, "Oh, it was just Colonel Nesbitt." She took a cigarette from a mother-of-pearl box on the coffee table and lit it with the matching lighter, glad that her fingers were so steady. She sat down on the couch.

Charlie sprawled in a wing chair opposite and expostulated, "Colonel *Nesbitt?* You mean the guy from this afternoon? Did you have dinner with him or something? What did he say, for God's sake? Are you going to get a flight? What's he like, Ma? Is he like one of those grouchy old guys in the comedies?"

Lisa had to laugh, even if she was uneasy about telling the story. "Which question should I answer first?"

Charlie laughed too. She was very good-natured about jokes against herself. "Sorry about that. Why don't you just tell it like it was...and I'll shut up."

Like it was, Lisa repeated silently. She wasn't about to do that. She paused, hating to lie to her daughter. But on the other hand she couldn't tell her what had actually happened, either. Certainly not yet. Lisa immediately analyzed the "yet." There might not *be* a yet.

"Ma?" Charlie prompted.

Lisa thought, I've got to say *something*.. "There's not that much to it," she began slowly. "First of all, I haven't definitely been promised a flight."

"Oh, wow! Not *'definitely'*? You mean you *could* get a flight!" Charlie was beaming.

"I thought you were going to let me tell it," Lisa reminded her gently, smiling.

"Sorry. But don't stop *now!"* Charlie made a face of mock pain.

"All right. When I saw Colonel Nesbitt this afternoon, he asked me to go to Houston to work on a problem they're having there."

Her daughter gasped, then put both hands over her mouth as if to keep herself from talking. Lisa chuckled, then went on. "I haven't said yes to that yet..." She burst out laughing. Charlie was pressing her hands to her mouth now and wriggling in the chair, obviously dying to comment. "And Colonel Nesbitt implied that he *might* be able to get me on a flight." Charlie looked as if she might burst, so Lisa kidded her, "Okay. Go!"

Charlie lowered her hands with a dramatic sigh and rushed into speech. "Why *can't* we go to Houston? Look, I can rearrange things with Dad, go up to the Cape later on. You can get Brenda to take care of the house—she always likes that, anyway—and turn over your patients to some other shrink! Oh, Ma, we've *got* to go!"

"Well, I hope you'll enjoy your new post...as administrator at NYU," Lisa twitted her a shade reproachfully.

"Oh, wow, I'm sorry. I didn't mean to come across like that," Charlie apologized. "But we can arrange it, can't we, Mother? Please. Do you realize I've never even *been* to Texas?"

Lisa thought, she always calls me Mother when she wants something. Then another thought, less amusing, came to her: when she'd contemplated going to Houston she'd somehow pictured herself alone there, with Nesbitt. She was assailed with fresh guilt.

Almost involuntarily she found herself saying, "Texas is delightful, but it's awfully hot this time of year. You'd be a lot more comfortable on the Cape."

As soon as she'd said it, Lisa hated herself. Charlie looked stricken. "You *are* thinking of going, Ma. And you'd rather I didn't. That's what it sounds like."

"I didn't mean it that way at all," Lisa protested. She got up and went to her daughter, bending down to kiss her nose. Charlie turned her face away, still looking hurt. Her long, corn-silk hair veiled her expression, but Lisa could see her mouth. It trembled.

"Charlie," Lisa coaxed her. "Come *on,* now." She brushed aside the silk skein of hair and stroked her daughter's cheek.

She straightened, pulling herself together. "Look, darling, it's not definite anyway. I was just talking about your comfort, that's all. Let us not forget," she said comically, "I *am* your mother."

Charlie looked brighter. "I know. I'm sorry I was such a baby."

Lisa smiled, feeling better. She went back to the couch and sat down again, realizing just how drained she felt.

"So what is he like, Ma...the colonel? Very uptight and official?"

Lisa thought, I've got to tell her. If they should meet each other, it would be the most horrendous shock...and then she would wonder why on earth I *didn't* tell her.

"Brace yourself," she said, smiling. "Colonel Nesbitt was that man we saw on the terrace." Lisa hoped her emotions weren't showing through.

"What!" Charlie's eyes looked as big as saucers; she was obviously flabbergasted. "I don't believe it. That gorgeous thing is a *colonel*?"

"Yes." Lisa was nobly controlling her voice. "And, in many ways, *very* 'uptight and official.'" She grinned at the still-amazed Charlie. "You see, one of the problems I'd have would be his bullheadedness. I think he's already decided on the answer to this technical problem and he just wants me there to be his yes-woman."

"But *Ma*...he's so good-looking. And you said he might be able to get you a flight."

"That's not certain at all," Lisa assured her.

"But first things first." Charlie's grin was impudent, incorrigible. "He's really gorgeous. He makes Greg look like something out of...a cemetery, for heaven's sake."

"Charlie."

"Well, I'm sorry, but it's true. Is he an Aries?"

"Now how would I know that?" Lisa hedged. With a sudden inspiration, she said hastily, "Speaking of astrology, I *love* that book. I got all the way through the first part. It's loads of fun."

Charlie was only half diverted. "I'm glad you like it; I think it's the greatest. But listen, Ma, don't change the subject on me. *Please*, let's go to Houston."

Lisa rose wearily. "Simmer down. I told you I'll think about it. Right now I'm going to have a shower and read awhile and go to sleep. It's been a day and a half."

"Okay." Charlie jumped up from the chair. She was always so agreeable, Lisa thought; that was one of the many things that made her so dear. Charlie came over and hugged her hard. "I do have the neatest mother," she murmured.

"My daughter's not too bad, either." Lisa hugged her back and kissed the top of her shining head. Then they went back into the hall after Lisa had turned off the lights, and she watched Charlie race up the stairs ahead of her.

She couldn't believe sometimes what a sweet child she had. Charlie rarely answered her back or gave her trouble.

She'd even left the bathroom neat and shining, Lisa discovered when she went in. It went without saying that Charlie had washed her hair—she did that every day—but everything was shipshape.

Lisa wandered back into her bedroom to undress. Returning to the bath in a thin cream-colored robe, she realized what she'd just done: any normal person undressed in the bedroom first, then went to bathe. She'd been in such an absentminded state that she'd gone right to the bath fully dressed.

She shook her head, staring at herself a moment in the mirror over the sink. Her eyes looked enormous and her mouth positively bee-stung...from Nesbitt's kiss? Surely Charlie had noticed that.

Lisa hung her robe on a hook and, pulling aside the shower curtain with its design of misty pastel flowers, turned the shower on. The rush of lukewarm water felt wonderful on her face and hair and body, and the full extent of her strange exhaustion struck her. She *never* felt this tired. Her health was extraordinarily good, practically perfect.

Fool, she admonished herself. A doctor—a psychiatrist, at that—should be aware of the effect of excitement and emotion. Both the prospect of rejoining NASA and the unbelievable time with Nesbitt had wrung her out like a washcloth. She just couldn't wait to stretch out in bed. Hurriedly she bathed and washed her hair.

She liked to dry it naturally instead of blowing it dry. It was short enough for that, and besides, at Lisa's age, natural drying helped preserve her hair's health and shine. So she just ran a comb through it and let it swing damply as she put on her robe again and went down the hall to Charlie's room.

The door was ajar. Her daughter looked up and smiled when she saw Lisa. She was wearing an enormous pink-and-blue-striped nightshirt and looked adorable. Her small TV set was on at low volume. "My TV bother you, Ma?"

"Not a bit. Good night, kiddo."

"'Night." Charlie blew her a kiss. "Think about Houston, will you?"

"You can bet I'll be thinking about it." Lisa waved and wandered back to her own room.

She discarded her robe, got into a nightgown and, with a sigh of utter relief, pulled back the spread and lay down in her wide platform bed. Annoyed, she realized that the interesting new novel was still downstairs, and she was too lazy to go get it. But she didn't really need a book right now. As she'd said to Charlie, she would definitely be thinking about Houston...and many, many other things. Her mind drifted to the past.

Lisa's earliest memories were of many different places, many new houses. As soon as she'd gotten used to one it was time to move to another. Her father, Philip Marley, the daring Flying Tiger, had been much decorated in World War II. Apart from a swift leave in 1943, when he'd been temporarily invalided out of combat, her father had not returned to the States until 1946. Lisa herself was the happy result of the one leave.

After the war Phil Marley, a brilliant scientist as well as soldier, joined the infant space industry in Huntsville, Alabama, at the Redstone Arsenal. Lisa was too young to remember much about Huntsville, but as time went on she came to know a variety of places—Houston, Texas; Cape Canaveral, Florida; Washington, D.C.; Baltimore, Maryland; and several other sites where the family moved, following the demands of her father's career.

By the time she was twelve, Lisa had resolved to imitate her father; even as a child she had an amazing grasp of mechanics. So when she was ready for college her delighted father sent her to MIT. While she was just a sophomore she met a handsome, exciting young intern who was visiting Boston—Jack Heron, attached to Columbia Presbyterian Hospital in New York City.

They fell madly in love and eloped, putting an end to her studies at MIT, because it was necessary for them to live in New York.

During the early years of the marriage, several things happened to Lisa Heron. Chief among them, she discovered that her young husband was not the man she'd fallen in love with. He had decided to specialize in plastic surgery, with an eye toward a lucrative cosmetic practice among the rich and famous. While there was nothing wrong with that, Lisa decided, it wasn't the noble kind of medicine she had envisioned.

Furthermore, her father and Jack disliked each other intensely. Her husband thought the whole space industry was just Buck Rogers nonsense. Lisa missed MIT sorely, too. When she became pregnant she decided to finish her engineering degree at night and pursued that for another year, right up to and just after the birth of her stillborn baby.

Things seemed to get worse and worse between her and Jack. And during that period the devastating accident occurred in Houston that resulted in the deaths of three astronauts, for which her father irrationally took the blame.

Phil Marley, when Lisa visited him, seemed to be going into a deeper and deeper depression. Soon his work began to suffer. Her father's condition inspired Lisa to become a psychiatrist. Against enormous odds, and with great difficulty, she got her MD and then interned in psychiatry.

She got her MD the same year Charlie was born. With the birth of their daughter, Jack and Lisa were drawn a bit closer together again, and Lisa decided that she'd try her best to make the marriage a success. But it was no good. Jack reproached Lisa for being an "unnatural woman" who was more interested in a career—and her father—than her husband and daughter.

While there might have been some justice for his assertion about himself, Jack was totally wrong about Lisa's lack of interest in her daughter. The baby grew into a happy, well-adjusted toddler, then a beautiful, intelligent child, under Lisa's care. In later years it positively exhausted Lisa to remember how she had coped with it all—her work, her child, her home and husband. And her father.

Five years ago Lisa and Jack had finally divorced. Her father, meanwhile, had resigned from the space program and become miserable doing utterly unrelated work in private industry. Then, four years ago, Phil Marley's long-suppressed guilt and years of depression had culminated in a total nervous breakdown. He'd been confined to a mental institution ever since.

Recently, however, he had been pronounced fit to be released in October. That was one reason Lisa wanted to stay in New York; she wanted to be on hand when her father came home. Her parents' home was now on Long Island.

But, Lisa thought, that's October...and this is June. Furthermore, her father had been overjoyed when she'd told him on a visit that she'd qualified as a mission specialist in the space program. And, as a matter of fact, the psychiatrist had told Lisa that he believed her association with the program had actually helped speed her father's recovery, that ultimately it could even lead him to rejoining the program himself. Lisa was well aware what a glorious thing that would be for him—for so many years it had been his whole life, and everyone she'd ever talked to about him had spoken in glowing terms of his inventive genius, and what a loss to the industry his absence had been.

Nesbitt, too, had been positively awed by Philip Marley.

Nesbitt.

Lisa tossed restlessly in bed, recalling the amazing thing that had happened between them—the sudden wild and stunning embrace, her own barbaric excitement, her melting, startled submission.

Analyzing her reluctance to enter the project with him, Lisa wondered if part of it could be fear. Maybe she just didn't want to rock her peaceful boat; maybe she was downright afraid to expose herself to pain and disappointment again. It was not an attractive image of herself—a woman who was afraid to start really living a second time.

In her seesaw fashion, her usual balancing and weighing, Lisa debated. A good part of what she felt was a reluctance to leave New York, the only home she'd ever had for any length of time. But that was silly. If she were assigned to a space flight, she'd have to leave in any case. Also, she'd love to work with Heinz.

And, as Charlie had pointed out, it could be done; Lisa's summer schedule wasn't engraved in marble. Her adaptable young colleague, Brenda, would jump at the chance to stay in the house, as she had before. Still looking for a Village apartment, Brenda was sharing with another woman in the East Thirties. She loved being able to walk to work and enjoy the Village atmosphere.

Initially, of course, it would be a tentative arrangement, because Lisa wouldn't know how long she'd be in Houston until she'd checked it out.

Good heavens, she was thinking of it as a fait accompli. But as long as she was thinking like that, she might as well go the whole way: Charlie's plans for the Cape weren't settled yet, either. None of Lisa's patients was fragile enough to be upset by a temporary change of therapist. Furthermore, Lisa admitted to herself, her desire to start the research project in late summer rather than in the fall, which would be more logical, had been a result of her compulsiveness...her need to mask an inner emptiness with unnecessary activity.

She recalled again what her father's psychiatrist had said: "Your own involvement in the space program may be the impetus your father needs to put him back where he belongs."

The bottom line was that she needed very little rationalization, that she was wildly eager to go. She knew just how long she'd been suppressing her yen for everything connected with space travel.

As far as Nesbitt was concerned—she was surprised that she'd ever thought she couldn't handle him. Or most things, for that matter. Any woman who had survived a marriage with Jack Heron, had a baby while she'd gotten a medical degree, and raised that baby to be a happy, healthy young woman, survived her father's breakdown and helped fill her mother's emptiness—well, a small matter like one more nervy, pushy man didn't count for much.

Hooray for the great Lisa Heron, she twitted herself. But how could it hurt to pat oneself on the back now and then? She'd accomplished plenty, and she'd only begun.

Now she was on fire with new enthusiasm; her adrenaline was rushing. By golly, they would go. And she'd tell Charlie right this minute. Her daughter wasn't asleep yet. Lisa could still hear the murmur of the TV.

She sprang up from the bed and padded down the hall barefoot to Charlie's room.

"Well, hi!" Charlie said, surprised. She lowered the TV. "What's up?"

"We're going to Houston."

"Oh, Ma!" Charlie jumped out of bed and ran to Lisa, hugging her so hard it hurt Lisa's ribs.

"Take it easy," Lisa said good-naturedly.

"I'm sorry." Charlie was grinning from ear to ear. "Now...when are we going? What'll I pack? How long are we going to stay?"

Lisa took her by the arm and led her firmly to the bed, where they plopped down together. "I would guess Sunday." Lisa said, "but I've got to check it out first. Right now I don't know how long it'll be, and as for packing..."

Charlie jumped up again and rushed to her closet.

Lisa laughed. *"Tonight?"*

Her daughter was half hidden among her clothes, and she mumbled something about taking an inventory.

"We shouldn't take much," Lisa warned her. "We may not be there that long. If it turns out we will be, Brenda can send things along, or we can get things in Houston. They've got the best boutiques, I hear."

Charlie emerged from the closet, beaming. "Oooh...that sounds wonderful."

Lisa finally got her settled down enough to tell her what Houston's weather was like, and fill her in as much as possible. She herself hadn't been there for three years. "It was mushrooming then," Lisa concluded, "so it's probably grown even more since I was there."

They chatted a long time, until even the energetic Charlie was sleepy.

"Enough?" Lisa asked.

"Oh, *yes.*" Charlie lounged back in bed, her eyelids heavy-looking.

"Let's get some sleep, then." Lisa switched off the TV set and rubbed the top of Charlie's head affectionately. "We've got a lot to do tomorrow." They had agreed that the department stores were a hassle on Saturday, and decided that they'd do a little shopping in the Village.

And Lisa had a lot of people to call. Fortunately most of her patients were scheduled from Wednesday through Friday, so there'd be sufficient time to reschedule them. Lisa would have to call them all personally at home, or at their weekend places, then get in touch with Nesbitt and take care of a variety of other things.

When she was back in her own room, she lay down thankfully and turned off her light. It was foolish, but she hoped Nesbitt wouldn't be in when she phoned, that she could just leave a message. She could ask him to leave directions on her answering machine.

"You're a coward, Lisa Heron," she mumbled as she drifted off to sleep.

Maybe so, she decided as drowsiness stole in. But she had the distinct feeling that she'd better avoid personal contact with him as much as possible: a man like Michael Nesbitt could be a threat to both her private and professional serenity.

Yet in spite of herself, half-dreaming, half-waking, she had the clearest picture of his tanned and reckless face, the stunning height and breadth of him, with that overpowering aura that said without apology, "I am a man."

Chapter 3

"I don't believe this plane, Ma. So this is what a VIP jet is like." Winging toward Houston on the following Sunday afternoon, Charlie and Lisa were leaning back in soft beige designer chairs, in the midst of a huge space that looked like a living room.

Lisa smiled. "This is it."

Nesbitt had gone forward to speak to the pilot about something, and Lisa was strangely relieved by his momentary absence. When he was with them he was so very *there,* she thought uneasily. She studied Charlie, who was looking out at the fleecy clouds beyond the window.

Her daughter was uncharacteristically soft-voiced and subdued, dazzled into quietness.

Anyone would be, Lisa conceded; they were both in a kind of time warp, since Lisa herself was slightly giddy from the rapid sequence of events during the past two days. She closed her eyes for a second, reviewing things.

Yesterday morning she and Charlie had awakened early. Charlie had been so excited that she'd started packing even before breakfast, and woken up a half-dozen friends to phone them the news. Finally, at eleven, it had been late enough in Lisa's estimation to call people on a Saturday morning.

As Charlie rushed off to her favorite boutiques on Eighth Street and Greenwich Avenue, Lisa began by calling Nesbitt first. To her vast relief he was out and she left her message. Then she made her other calls. By the time she'd gotten everything arranged to her satisfaction and been assured that her patients would not be disturbed by her absence, it was almost time for lunch.

She was preparing it when Charlie rushed in with several shopping bags containing a new two-piece outfit to travel in, a new bikini and thin cotton trousers. Then Charlie rushed out again to say goodbye to "some people," promising to be back for dinner. Lisa halted her, got more details, and ate half of the lunch she'd fixed.

Later she decided to get her hair cut and shop for something special for dinner. Brenda would be joining them, to visit and pick up the keys for tomorrow. Lisa hadn't even heard from Nesbitt yet about when they'd leave, but she thought it was safe to assume that it would be Sunday, since he'd been so anxious.

When she returned from the hairdresser's and the market, a message was on her tape machine...Nesbitt's brazen, exultant message: "A-Okay, lady. I'll have a car in front of your door at one tomorrow afternoon. How about dinner tonight? Will you call me?"

Lisa remembered how her heartbeat had quickened when she heard his voice. She called back. He was gone again, and once more she left a message that Sunday was fine, but that she had other plans for dinner that night. It was absolutely craven, she thought, to be so glad that circumstances had taken it out of her hands—that she could leave a civil but impersonal message instead of having to talk to him.

Immediately after that she'd asked herself what she was going to do when she *had* to talk with him, to work with him, work with him closely.

But there had been so much to do that she had been able to forget about that for a while. Charlie had decided to have dinner with a friend, but had promised to come home early. Lisa finished her dinner preparations and packing, and had a pleasant time with Brenda. Charlie kept her word and came home at eleven, and they both slept like hibernating bears, tired out from rushing around and getting ready.

Late Sunday morning there had been a last-minute flurry and a lovely breakfast that Brenda had cooked for them, then the arrival of Mike Nesbitt and the limousine.

Encountering him again, Lisa realized how happy she was that Charlie was going. Throughout the ride to the airport and as they boarded the VIP plane, her daughter's presence kept him at a discreet distance.

And seeing him reenter the cabin now, Lisa was sharply aware of just how convenient that could be, as he turned that vivid blue gaze upon her, opening her up all over again to turbulent emotions.

Michael Nesbitt's eyes met her soft brown ones when he stepped into the cabin, and he thought how lovely she was. It didn't seem possible, but she was more beautiful than she'd been before, in that sleek dress the color of her hair.

His glance flicked to her daughter. The kid was as bright as a cockatoo, in a red, blue and yellow dress. As a matter of fact, her funny hairdo, all up on top of her head, reminded him of a bird's crest. At first, when he'd heard she was going, too, he'd been pretty annoyed. So much for a nice long trip for two. But after he'd talked to her a little, he couldn't help liking her; she was both smart and amusing.

After all, the kid couldn't be left alone. But still, for the first time in his unconflicted life, Nesbitt was impatient and conflicted as hell.

No woman had ever hit him so hard or so fast as Lisa Heron. He could no more have stopped himself from kissing her that night than he could have stopped a sneeze. Yet he knew that of all the women he could want, she was the last one he should have chosen.

If he needed her as a man, he needed her even more as a colleague. The whole project might depend on her. He was lucky he hadn't blown it already by grabbing her like that the other night. It was a minor miracle. He was going to keep his cool if it killed him, really watch himself from now on. It had taken every ounce of his control not to call her again the night before. But her cool little message about "other plans" had given him the message of "Back off, buddy."

Now her polite half smile, her pointed look away, tipped him off to the fact that it was time to say something, not just stand there staring like a dumb gorilla. He glanced at the heavy chronometer on his wrist, amazed but gratified that he'd had so many thoughts in so few seconds. Time had gone by with the speed of a training jet since he'd walked in. But then, the time had gone by like that with her ever since Day One.

Nesbitt came to and managed to say in a calm, friendly tone, "We'll land right on schedule, three CST. I was checking out which airport we'll be using. I figured if it was HIA instead of Hobby, I'd get a copter, since HIA is farther."

"Is it like New York?" Charlie demanded. "Two hours in the air and four on the ground?"

Nesbitt chuckled. "Just about. I've radioed for a copter."

"Ooooh, good. I've never been in one," Charlie enthused.

Lisa smiled and said to Nesbitt, "I haven't been to Houston in a while. I guessed it's changed."

Nesbitt sat down in a chair opposite her. Fighting against the visual distraction of her neat golden hair, her flawless skin and inviting features, he agreed and began to describe the current state of the city.

"It's a real 'asphalt jumble,'" he punned for the interested Charlie. She was taking in everything he said with breathless attention, giving him melting looks from her big blue-gray eyes, and Nesbitt wondered uneasily if the kid was getting a crush on him. He didn't need any more complications. "Houston's growing so fast that the photographers have to shoot new postcards twice a year just to keep up with the skyline."

He glanced at Lisa. She was listening politely, with a pleasant expression, but still very much at a distance. Nesbitt was bound and determined to get her alone as soon as he could. He'd go nuts if he couldn't talk to her in private and try to gauge what she felt about what had happened Friday night.

"Are there cowboys?" Charlie demanded.

"Just ones from Dallas that play football; they play at the Astrodome occasionally," he kidded. "Sure," he said more seriously, "there are cowboys, but you'll find them farther out of town. As a matter of fact, some friends of mine have a big spread in the area. And they've got some kids about your age."

"Will you take us there? Can I ride?"

"Don't push, Charlie," Lisa warned softly.

"Of course I'll take you," Nesbitt assured Charlie, smiling at Lisa with a that's-okay expression.

His heart did a slow roll when he saw the warm, grateful look in those velvety eyes, and he lost track of what he'd been saying.

"I think you've cross-examined the colonel enough, kiddo," Lisa said with that flippant mildness that Nesbitt admired. She always seemed to know just the right tone to take with her daughter.

Charlie giggled. "I guess I have. Sorry if I was a pest, Colonel Nesbitt."

He hastened to reassure her, but was glad all the same to knock off the travelogue. With Lisa Heron this close he was having a hell of a time putting two consecutive thoughts together.

The girl picked up a magazine and started to leaf through it. Lisa closed her eyes, leaning back.

Free to watch her now, Nesbitt enjoyed the sight of her chiseled profile, the sweep of her long brown lashes on her satiny cheeks, her faintly tilted nose and small, neat mouth. It looked like a...rosebud.

His skin felt sticky under his shirt, and he shifted in his chair, remembering how that mouth had tasted, recalling the feel of her slender body in his arms.

Damn. If he sat there looking at her any longer, unable to touch her, to kiss her, he'd have to smash something. Murmuring, "Excuse me," he got up and went forward again. Maybe he'd feel better talking to the pilot.

By the time they touched down in Houston, he was calmer. At least now he'd be able to move; there'd be things to take care of.

He helped the women disembark and got them and their gear into the copter, sympathizing with their reaction to the heat. As usual, Charlie had a thousand questions, and he pointed out some highlights of the city, including Tranquillity Park, commemorating the Apollo space flights; the seventy-five-story Texas Commerce Tower; and Allied Bank Plaza, fifty floors of brilliant reflective glass.

"Wow! It's a real *city!*" Charlie was thrilled.

Nesbitt grinned at her and glanced at Lisa. Even in this garish light, he thought, she was absolutely gorgeous. A perfect woman.

"They'll set us down right next door to the Golden Seasons," Nesbitt said.

"The Golden Seasons?" Lisa protested. "Look here, Colonel Nesbitt, that's a bit much, don't you think?" Occupying one full block in the new Houston Center, the hotel was the very finest in the city, and fabulously expensive. "I really think we should..." She hesitated. It was an awkward time, she thought, to bring up the matter of paying her own expenses. "I really think we'd be more comfortable in something less...elaborate," she resumed in a firm tone.

"Well, let's talk about it later," he responded easily. "The powers that be want you to have VIP treatment."

He glanced at Charlie and imagined a mutinous expression on her pretty face, a kind of why not in her lifted eyebrows. He repressed a chuckle. He had *one* ally, at least, in this conspiracy to spoil her mother.

"All right," Lisa murmured, but she still didn't look satisfied. This lady was going to be a tough nut to crack, Nesbitt decided. And yet he couldn't help admiring her independence.

They were exposed to the blistering heat for only a very short time as they moved from the air-conditioned executive copter to an air-conditioned car that drove them to the entrance of the fabulous Golden Seasons. As the three walked in, coolness was already apparent, washing out from the enormous lobby with carpeting so deep that walking was like wading. Only this, Nesbitt judged, was good enough for Lisa Heron.

She registered, and Nesbitt said, "I thought you'd enjoy a garden room on the fourth floor. The swimming pool's there, with the whirlpool and the sun deck."

Lisa raised her graceful brows as Charlie cried out, "Oh, Colonel Nesbitt...it sounds terrific!"

He laughed. "I must admit, it *is*."

A vividly uniformed attendant led them to the refined elegance of the elevator, and they were spirited soundlessly to the beautiful fourth floor, which seemed like a small resort in itself.

Their suite had a living room with a bedroom on either side, and boasted bay windows overlooking the city, fresh flowers and custom-made furniture. Charlie was too dazzled to speak, but Lisa Heron said politely, "This is really lovely."

"I'm glad you like it." Nesbitt tipped the attendant before Lisa could open her bag, and added, "I'll leave you ladies to get settled. What do you say to a night out on the town a little later...say about seven? I'd love to show your daughter one of the spiffier places. May I?"

When he put it like that it was sheer blackmail, and he knew Lisa couldn't graciously refuse. And a two-hour flight was hardly cause for pleading tiredness. He saw those thoughts mirrored in her beautiful, reluctant eyes.

"That would be very kind of you," she said.

"Wonderful!" He was feeling great now. "I'll call for you here at seven."

With one more long look at her, and a friendly wave to Charlie, Nesbitt left the suite.

Standing in the luxurious shower, Lisa thought about how lovely the hotel was. The shower head was at the perfect height, and she was lathering herself with the French-milled soap that had been provided. There was even some quality shampoo on the porcelain shelf.

She washed her hair again, although she had washed it just last night, deciding that she'd soon be as bad as Charlie, shampooing twice a day. When she finished she stepped onto the fuzzy wall-to-wall green rug that looked like grass and dried herself with an enormous towel that felt as soft as velvet.

Charlie had already bathed and was dressing. Lisa went back to her room, shaking her slightly damp hair, and debated what to wear. When Nesbitt had specified one of the "spiffier" places, Lisa knew that meant real dressing up. Houston was a moneyed, glamorous town. She'd already told Charlie that.

She'd brought only a few things that were really right for evening, and she decided on the most elaborate one, a thin chenillelike velvet of ombreé creams and taupes and beiges printed at one shoulder with stylized black and russet flowers. She slipped it on, adding a cuff bracelet of pewter and tarnished copper, and big drop earrings of pewter and brown cat's-eye stones.

The brown gems exactly matched her eyes, and the tawny colors of the dress made her pale tan glow, investing her blond hair with striking splendor.

Damned good for an old girl like me, she concluded, looking at the result in the mirror. She wondered why she was taking such extraordinary care and answered silently, because this is Houston and I want Charlie to be proud of me.

Balderdash. She had to face the fact that she was doing it for Michael Nesbitt. And knowing that, she was assailed with fresh anxiety. She was playing right into his hands.

It was painfully obvious that he was trying to buy her, as well as make love to her. The VIP treatment, the outrageously expensive hotel, the blithe promise of a flight, even his extraspecial niceness with Charlie, were all a part of the package, the outright blackmail. And his prize would be her concurrence with his diagnosis of the situation at the center.

"Well, look at *you.*" Glancing up, Lisa saw Charlie reflected in her mirror. She looked lovely in a short aqua silk dress with a bright pink sash.

"And you, too," Lisa retorted, smiling back at Charlie. She turned around. "I love that dress." The colors made Charlie's hair shine like a gold piece, and turned her blue-gray eyes as blue as...Michael Nesbitt's.

That comparison filled her with such consternation that it must have showed on her face, because Charlie asked, "What's wrong, Ma?"

"Not a thing," she said lightly. "As long as you approve of your haggard old mother," she kidded.

Charlie giggled. "You're gorgeous. And Colonel Nesbitt thinks so, too. He really likes you. That's great.... He's the neatest man. He reminds me of the heroes in old war movies."

Lisa started to say something about books and their covers, but thought better of it. Why bring it up now and spoil her daughter's evening? It was obvious that Charlie had a harmless crush on him, and it had never been Lisa's style to dash cold water over anything. She hated the idea of upset and unpleasantness.

"He does, a bit," Lisa said calmly and, to distract her, added, "It's nearly seven."

Almost as soon as the words were out of her mouth, the bedroom extension buzzed. Lisa answered, and was informed that Colonel Nesbitt was asking for them.

She told the man to send him up, and went to get her bag and silky cream jacket. "Better take your coat," she called out to Charlie.

Charlie went to get it, saying agreeably, "I read you, Houston."

Lisa went to answer the door as Charlie came out of her own room with her thin, short-sleeved coat over her arm.

This was still another Mike Nesbitt. He looked more formal than she'd seen him so far, in a summer suit of a blue so dark it was almost black.

He stared down at her, not saying a word. Finally he smiled, murmuring, "You look—" As she stood aside to let him in, he concluded "—gorgeous. Both of you," he added quickly, catching sight of Charlie. "They lied."

"Who lied?" Lisa asked with a sudden feeling of gaiety.

"Everybody who said the prettiest women come from Texas. I think they come *to* Texas."

Oh, dear, he's awfully smooth, Lisa was thinking as he escorted them to the elevator and into the lobby. Charlie had reacted very strongly to his pretty compliment.

He handed them into a neat black Mercedes, saying casually, "I thought you might like to go to Toby's for dinner tonight...to make the transition more gradual."

"How nice," Lisa said. She explained to Charlie, "It's a really 'uptown' place." As a matter of fact, Toby's was so spectacular that Lisa connected it with extraordinary celebrations. Nesbitt was really courting her...or them...and the idea excited her in spite of her resolve to keep cool with him. This, too, could be part of a sharp maneuver.

But when Toby Vallon himself greeted them and made a great fuss over his friend Mike's guests, Lisa couldn't help being delighted, and Charlie was overwhelmed by the antique Chinese screens and wine-colored walls, the tuxedoed waiters and the fresh flowers everywhere.

Nesbitt said, "Their grilled veal chops are sensational, but they've got some great pasta that's not on the menu." He consulted with the captain very seriously on Charlie's behalf, as if, Lisa decided with amusement, he were checking out a vehicle before a flight. After much consultation they decided.

The meal *was* wonderful, and he was obviously knocking himself out to entertain them with funny stories. Lisa was touched by that, and she was very aware of the way other women covertly admired him, even in this place full of handsome, well-dressed men. She was aware of something else, too—his vivid eyes returned again and again to her, admiring her and seeming to ask for her approval.

They finished the meal with an ambrosial raspberry soufflé and sat a long time over coffee. Since the elaborate meal hadn't been served until after eight, it was already ten-thirty.

"Where to now?" Nesbitt asked genially. "I'm afraid it's too late for the theater, but maybe you feel like seeing a movie."

Charlie, whose eyelids looked heavy, said, "I'm ashamed to admit it, but I'm *sleepy.*"

"It's the change in weather," Lisa told her. "And you were up late last night." To Nesbitt, she said, "This is really lovely, but maybe we'd better go back to the hotel, Colonel."

"On one condition. That you stop with this 'Colonel' business and call me by my name. Mike. Both of you, okay?"

"Okay," Charlie agreed fervently, and Lisa nodded. She wished she could stop being so skeptical and relax a little. But she just couldn't. Tomorrow they'd have to stop all these pleasant overtures and get down to some really serious—perhaps troublesome—business.

The idea preoccupied her all the way back to the hotel. When they stopped before the entrance it seemed to her that Mike Nesbitt said with a forced casualness, "Oh, by the way, Lisa, there are a couple of things I'd like to talk to you about before tomorrow morning...Charlie, too."

"What's that?"

"First of all, how about giving Charlie the tour tomorrow at the center, while we're going about our business?"

"I'd like that," Charlie said, and Lisa agreed it was a good idea.

"Good. Meet me at the copter site at eight, then, if that's not too early."

"Eight's fine. If you have some other things to discuss, why don't you come up to the suite?" Lisa invited.

"I'd hate to disturb Charlie." That seemed to be a pretty weak excuse, Lisa thought. They could have bowled in the living room without disturbing her daughter. "Maybe you and I could have a nightcap somewhere...."

"All right." Lisa wondered why she was so reluctant. She knew she had to be polite and cooperative. He was still the one who could help her get a flight. But she knew she was fooling herself; she was downright nervous about being alone with him again. Nevertheless she gave Charlie a light good-night kiss and waited while Nesbitt saw her into the lobby and onto the elevator.

When he came back Lisa thought he looked elated. He got in, shut the car door and turned to her eagerly. "How about a nice, quiet piano bar?"

"I really couldn't eat or drink another thing," she protested. He stared at her a second, and his expression grew even more elated.

"Fine. Let's drive a little."

Lisa was silent, wondering how she'd let this happen...*why* she had. Facing the truth, she concluded that she'd wanted to be alone with him again, that she hadn't forgotten the feel of his arms, the taste of his mouth that evening in New York. She was afraid that she might have communicated this to him, because she sensed an expectancy in him, and his breath had quickened. She saw a slight smile on his lips, a fiery light in his eyes when she glanced at him and studied his strong face illuminated by the passing traffic.

They were on Clinton Drive now, heading east out of town. She remembered that this was the way to the wharves. Even though Houston was fifty miles inland from the Gulf, it was the country's third largest port. There was a forty-foot-deep ship channel dug through shallow Galveston Bay, up Buffalo Bayou. And there were many ships in the basin. She'd always enjoyed visiting this area. Nesbitt drove through Gate 8 and braked in a shadowy spot on the wharf.

She was almost disconcerted when he didn't turn to her at once. He sat there looking dreamily out over the water, and remarked softly, "Do you happen to remember that old sci-fi show on TV...where the starship captain said that flying in space was like standing at the helm of a ship, feeling the wind from the sea?"

This was the last thing on earth Lisa had expected. She was teased by it, yet somehow very touched. "Yes, I do," she murmured. "I loved it."

"Well, Lisa Heron," he said, turning to her and looking at her earnestly, "the first time I saw you I had just that feeling. I was absolutely flying; I was swinging on the Peter Pan."

She stared into his eyes, bubbling with giddy laughter over his reference to the "Peter Pan," a weird, trapezelike contraption that helped astronauts in training feel the effects of spacewalks. She felt like she'd been hanging on to one herself just now and had just let go.

Their faces were very close. He whispered almost against her lips, "This is the first time in two whole days we've been unchaperoned." He raised his hands to cup her shoulders. "I had the best feeling tonight...that I was getting the go signal from mission control."

So he *had* read her. She couldn't speak; she felt dizzy now with his nearness. She could only wait for his hungry mouth to reach hers, then give herself up to the kiss she too had so desperately wanted.

He kissed her as if they hadn't touched each other in a long, long time, and a shock of excitement overpowered her.

While she was still able to think, a wild, strange idea came to her from nowhere: she was always trying to get her patients to face the truth in themselves, and she herself, the healer, had been unable to heal herself...had been totally unwilling to face her own truth. The fact was that she wanted Mike Nesbitt, wanted him more than any man she had ever known.

She was weak with longing now and slid her arms around his sinewy neck, drawing his head closer so she could return in full measure the savage pressure of his mouth. She felt his muscular hands on her breasts, then stroking her sides, caressing her narrow waist. Her own shaky hands touched his cheeks, his ears and his short, stubbly hair that teased her fingertips. The feel of it brought on a fresh tremor of excited desire deep within her, and her quivering fingers roamed downward tenderly to stroke the hot skin of his neck.

When their lips parted for a second, she heard him whisper, gasping, "Oh, Lisa, Lisa, you don't know how I've wanted this."

His touch was hot and urgent on her breasts. She moaned with a pleasure that was half assent and half protest, feeling his hands descending to her thighs. She was lost.

Lost.

The somber word rang clear in her mind, and her instincts shouted foolishly in space language, Signal Red, Signal Red.

Freeing her mouth, she said, breathless, "No, Mike. No. We can't do this."

His body shocked into stillness, he dropped his hands from her throbbing flesh. "What...what did you say, Lisa?"

She pulled away from him, moving to the other side of the seat. "I said we can't do this, Mike."

"What do you mean? Why not? Lisa, are you trying to tell me you don't want this as much as I do? What are you saying?" he demanded, trying to take her into his grasp again.

"I'm saying," she responded sadly, "that I don't trust you, Mike. I can't. This has all happened too fast for me.... There are too many other...things in the balance here."

She looked at him. His face expressed a kind of baffled anger, a frustrated pain. "I'm sorry," she said softly. "It can't happen. Not now."

"Why can't it?" he persisted. "We're grown-up people. We both want this. I know damned well I do, and from the way you kissed me, Lisa, so do you. You're not some kid who can't make up her mind."

"That's just the problem, I guess," she admitted somberly. "I'm not kid enough anymore to take everything on trust. By the time a woman gets to my age, she's more cautious...less fools-rush-in."

"That's nonsense, and you know it. Your age is my age, and I feel like...like this is the first time I've ever wanted a woman in my life." He reached out a tentative hand and touched her chin.

In spite of herself, she trembled at the light caress, was overwhelmed with tenderness to hear the declaration. But she shook her head, took a deep, shuddering breath and said flatly, "I don't know whether you're romancing me or my decision."

He jerked his hand away as if she'd burned him, and she heard him mutter a quiet, almost indistinguishable oath. "What a mind you have, Dr. Heron," he said roughly, and his voice sounded harsh, no longer titillating and exultant. "I might have known a shrink would analyze everything to death."

She was suddenly furious. "Don't take that tone with me."

He was apologetic in an instant. "Oh, Lord, I'm sorry. Look, I..."

But she couldn't be appeased that easily. "Take me back to the hotel, please."

He stared at her, then, swearing again under his breath, started the car and shot away. They made the brief trip in sullen silence, and he dropped her off at the hotel with a muttered "See you at eight." She nodded once, then fled into the lobby without looking back.

Charlie was apparently asleep when Lisa got back to the suite and began to prepare for bed with savage swiftness, feeling alternately annoyed and hurt, regretful and justified. It was maddening. Even more maddening was the fact that she lay awake for a long, long time, puzzling over the complex situation.

The next morning the weather report promised a bright, hot day. To calm herself, as much as for coolness, Lisa put on a shadowy plaid cotton dress with a companion shirt-jacket, and reflected that the quiet cocoa, rose and aqua combination actually soothed her. She put on a wide-brimmed cocoa straw hat. Besides being shelter from the sun, it would afford a handy screen for her shadowed eyes and somber expression. Besides, a hat for some reason seemed to express authority—it had worked that way for her before in sticky situations—and she'd need every bit of authority she could get today.

Charlie seemed so intent on the prospective tour of the space center that she was blessedly unaware of Lisa's nervous distraction. After a big breakfast, which Lisa just picked at, they met Nesbitt at the copter site.

He was more impressive than ever, Lisa decided with exasperation; in his uniform he looked easy and at home in the brilliant sun that didn't even make him squint.

Lisa greeted him with all the poise she could muster and slipped on big dark glasses. On the thirty-mile flight to the center he seemed to make a point of indifferent heartiness, pointing out various sights to Charlie.

When they landed at the center and Charlie caught sight of its sprawling white vastness, she commented, "This is pure sci-fi!" Nesbitt resumed his role of guide with an amiable answer, making Lisa feel glum and oppressive.

But her spirits couldn't help rising after they'd dispatched Charlie on her tour and were walking the familiar path to the admin building, their slang for administration. Nesbitt was quiet again, having abandoned the cheerful front he'd put up for Charlie's benefit.

Lisa looked at him. He was staring straight ahead, and his tough profile was grim and forbidding. She felt the same wretched confusion she'd experienced the night before, then a swift, irrational resentment against him for putting her in this position—though she had really put herself there.

But she had to say something, had to put this on a calm, businesslike basis. "It was awfully nice of you to set up the tour for Charlie."

"No trouble at all." His response was cool, neutral. He spoke with the politeness he'd show to any other colleague.

She went on nervously, "I'm looking forward to seeing Dieter Heinz again. We're old friends and associates."

He glanced aside at her for the first time and smiled. "Really? That's very nice."

Lisa mistrusted the words, suspected his tone and encouraged expression. Did he actually think she'd automatically agree with Heinz's conclusions? She was about to speak when they reached the entrance and went in. Her skin tightened in reaction to the chilly indoor air. But was it only the air, she wondered. And then she stopped short.

A burly uniformed officer was approaching them. He was apparently the welcoming committee. Her heart sank. Their official greeter was none other than Maj. James F. Rayburn, the one who'd given her such a rough time during the interviews when she'd gone through her training three years before.

There was a sarcastic glint in his flinty gray eyes and a tight little smile on his thin lips, as if it hurt him to look pleasant. "Well, well, Dr. Heron," he droned in his nasal voice. "Have a nice trip? Mike get you settled in all right?"

"Yes to both questions, Major." Lisa made herself smile and forced warmth into her answer. When she happened to glance at Mike Nesbitt she noticed a strange gleam in his cobalt eyes, a twisted grin on his lips.

"I want to thank *you,* Jim, for the splendid data you gave me on...New York." Nesbitt's tone was very peculiar, and Lisa wondered just what was behind it. There was an uncomfortable tension between the two men, and it didn't help her growing nervousness.

"Don't mention it, Mike." There was something unpleasant, she decided, in Rayburn's reply, in his mocking look.

"Oh, I *will*, Jim, again and again." What was going on here, she wondered. "Well," Nesbitt said briskly, "shall we go in? I'm sure the brass is waiting."

"That they are. Doctor?" Major Rayburn put a gingerly guiding hand on the small of Lisa's back. From him the gesture was condescending, not polite, and she felt her hackles rise. She moved slightly forward, and she and Rayburn followed Nesbitt into a huge consulting room where she saw more brass assembled than she'd ever seen in one place.

She felt positively intimidated until one of them, a genial-looking old man with a wild mane of gray hair, stood up, smiling. "Lisa! Lisa, darling." Dieter Heinz hurried to her and kissed her on the cheek.

Heartened, she thought, I've got one ally, anyway.

The rest of the day, full and hectic, fairly flew by. After the difficult conference with the skeptical administrative officers, Lisa had a clearer picture of the various hostilities and alliances. Rayburn, as she might have expected, detested Heinz, and had even less use for her. His comments on psychiatry bordered on the insulting, and it was clear that he thought his own astronaut team was far more competent than Nesbitt's. He had even tried to imply that Nesbitt's seeking her help was a political move to throw a smokescreen over his team's inability to "cut it."

Several times Rayburn tried to shake her when she offered the group her plan of investigation, but she hadn't let him, and was immensely proud of that fact. Inwardly fuming, she still managed to keep quite calm. Now and then she'd noticed that Dr. Heinz was hiding his triumphant amusement with difficulty.

The engineering personnel, as usual, were far easier to deal with. She recalled what her father had once said, "Scientists have ideas, but engineers make ideas live." Nesbitt and the engineering team engaged in a long and severely technical discussion; they were still hard at work on the problem of this mysterious new pogo and, surprisingly, were far more amenable than the administrative officers to the value of a psychological investigation.

Finally, after an exhausting harangue that lasted four full hours, it was agreed that Dr. Lisa Heron and Dr. Dieter Heinz would be empowered to pursue their investigation.

Mike Nesbitt disappeared somewhere when the group adjourned for lunch. Lisa and Dieter Heinz lunched together in a staff dining room, and were soon deep into discussion of their plans.

With a start of guilt Lisa suddenly thought of Charlie, and mentioned her to Heinz. He raised his shaggy gray brows, and his deep-set black eyes twinkled. "Lisa, your daughter is now seventeen, is she not?"

"She'll be eighteen in December."

"Ah!" Heinz grinned mischievously. "She is a young woman, then, not a child. Do you not think she will be all right for a little while without mama in attendance?"

Lisa flushed, thinking of her advice to Mrs. Prentice. "Touché," she said with chagrin. She knew she was overreacting to everything right now, simply because she was so sleep-deprived and anxious. What with the complexities of this project, the skepticism of Rayburn and the other administrators, and the situation with Nesbitt, she had an awful lot on her plate. "Dieter, you're absolutely right," she confessed.

"Good." He always pronounced that word like the German *gut*, she recognized with all her old affection. They had known each other for a long time; he'd been one of her professors when she was studying medicine, and was an old friend of her father's. "I'm sure you will conduct this study with all the brilliance I remember," he added.

Immediately after lunch they went to his office and began to set up a tentative schedule for the interviews with the astronaut team, which were to start the following morning. It began to look as if the project would take, even conservatively, anywhere from three weeks to a month. First there would be the interviews and tests, then an evaluation of those. Furthermore, Lisa planned to observe performance tests in various simulators and work with the engineers. Heinz, whose educational background was extraordinary, and included a knowledge of many scientific subjects, heartily concurred with the latter proposals.

Lisa thought, amused, that's why Dieter gets away with murder at those conferences—he's second only to Philip Marley. The thought of her father moved her for an instant to distracted tenderness, but she sternly brought her attention back to business.

Before she knew it, it was five-thirty, and Charlie was coming into the office, smiling from ear to ear, full of excited reports on her day.

"Good heavens!" Heinz exclaimed. "Some fairy godmother has turned you into a beautiful young woman, overnight."

Lisa was elated at Charlie's pleasure, and as they left the center, she still glowed with that, and with the familiar hominess of working with Heinz. Her doubts began to fade, and she was newly enthusiastic about the whole thing.

But she couldn't help noticing that Mike Nesbitt was nowhere to be seen. Charlie informed her with the charming self-importance of someone in the know that "Mike" had arranged for a "bubble" to take them back to Houston.

Trying to put Nesbitt out of her mind, Lisa got very busy that night—phoning Brenda with a request to send more clothes, going over their budget with Charlie to gauge their limit on shopping, and finding a very special restaurant for dinner.

One of their first orders of business, Lisa decided, would be to find a more moderate hotel. Staying in this palace for a month would be utter madness. She knew quite well what the straitened budget of the space program allowed, and she had an uneasy feeling that their hotel tab might be coming out of Nesbitt's pocket. Now, more than ever, that was an awkward matter. She resolved to see about that the first thing in the morning, and pay the Golden Seasons bill herself.

After dinner they took in a Houston Pops concert at Jones Hall, in the striking Tranquillity Park. The hall was open only during performances, but as Lisa said to Charlie, it was worth the price of admission just to see its insides. Charlie gasped, eyeing the fabulous sculpture *Gemini II* by Richard Lippold reaching into the upper reaches of the lobby.

Thousands of hexagonal rods, some as long as six feet, and each polished to a gemlike luster, were suspended from the ceiling by stainless-steel wire. Not one of the rods touched another; the magnificent piece seemed to echo and sing, following the angles and curves of the building.

The music was even more thrilling. Lisa was almost too moved by it; it was so poignant at times that she felt a tremor of cold pain deep within her. She knew that Mike Nesbitt had opened doors that had been closed for longer than she'd known.

When they returned to the hotel and walked through the fabulous lobby, Lisa remarked, "You'd better take advantage of the sun deck and pool tomorrow, honey. If we're going to be here for weeks, we're going to have to stay someplace a little less like the Taj Mahal."

She was pleasantly surprised when Charlie made a minimum of protest. "That's okay, Ma. Really. Just being in Houston and seeing the center is so fabulous. It's the most gorgeous place I've ever seen in my life. And Mike's going to take us out to that ranch this weekend. Believe me, there's more to Houston than this hotel."

Lisa was gratified to hear the new maturity in Charlie's voice. She hoped it didn't have too much to do with Mike Nesbitt. Charlie obviously idolized him, and Lisa was afraid she was going to be disillusioned sooner or later.

As they stepped out of the elevator, Lisa added silently, just the way I myself might be. She couldn't for the life of her plot his next maneuver.... The ranch expedition, for one, might be a device to get her daughter out of town.

Chapter 4

I hate to leave you here alone all day," Lisa said to Charlie the next morning.

Her daughter cocked an ironic eye at Lisa. "Don't you trust me to warm up my own formula?"

Lisa laughed out loud at that. "That's one for me."

"I can do a hundred things without even leaving this hotel—I'll be swimming and sunning, and nosing around the boutiques, and I'll probably take in the movie downstairs—or my favorite soaps—while you're slaving out there in the desert."

"Speaking of work...I'd better get going." Lisa got up from the breakfast table. "The copter will be taking off in about ten minutes." She'd checked the schedules the night before. It seemed the best way to commute for the time being, until she decided whether or not she'd rent a car.

She kissed Charlie on the top of her head. "Have fun. I may give you a call a little later. You know where to get me—in Heinz's office."

At the center she was pleased that Dieter Heinz wasn't in yet. They were temporarily sharing his office until hers was set up. She had quite a lot to think about and could do it better in solitude. For one thing, she couldn't let her personal feelings for Mike Nesbitt get her all distracted from the project.

She took her papers from her briefcase and plunged into study. She was deep in a psychological profile when the phone rang.

"Dr. Heron," she answered.

"Sergeant Fowler, ma'am." It was a very military voice, with a trace of Deep-South accent. "Aide to Colonel Nesbitt. The colonel asked me to inquire if everything is A-Okay so far and to inform you that your own office will be assigned to you about eleven."

His *aide*. She was a little miffed that he hadn't called himself, that he was playing the busy, high-powered officer.

"Dr. Heron?"

She rushed into speech. "Everything is...fine, Sergeant, and eleven will be quite satisfactory."

"Very good. And ma'am, someone will be along soon with your gear—your ID badge and a size-six lab coat. Is that right?"

Nesbitt has quite an eye for ladies' dress sizes, she thought. "Quite right, Sergeant Fowler. Thank you."

"Would there be anything else, ma'am?" If there were any such thing as a brisk drawl, this Sergeant Fowler had one, she decided.

"Yes, as a matter of fact there is. It's about my hotel accommodations. Could you tell me who would handle a change of quarters for the center?"

"You find your quarters *unsatisfactory,* ma'am?" The sergeant, military as he was, couldn't hide his surprise. Lisa didn't wonder; the Golden Seasons was the epitome of glamor.

"Not in the least," she assured him. "I was thinking of finding something less...elaborate for my stay."

There was a moment of puzzled silence, but then the sergeant rose to the occasion and replied crisply, "If you'll hold on just a second, ma'am, and let me check our records..."

She murmured assent, thinking there was an almost unreal quality about all the "ma'ams." But it occurred to her that professional personnel were equivalent to commissioned officers in the armed services.

In an amazingly short time the sergeant was back. "Ma'am, I think there's some misunderstanding here. According to my record your accommodations have already been taken care of until the end of the summer, at the Morland Hotel."

"I see." She was flabbergasted. "Well, thank you, Sergeant, I'll...pursue this at another time."

He rang off with spit-and-polish.

Lisa leaned back in her chair, digesting this information. She knew very well that the space program was on such a straitened budget that it would never approve such an extravagant expenditure. That meant Mike Nesbitt must be picking up the tab, disguising her hotel as the Morland, a far less expensive but quite elegant hostel in itself. The sergeant would *really* have been shocked if he'd known she was "objecting" to the Golden Seasons.

What a situation. She wondered if Nesbitt might be an alias—picking up the bill at the Seasons would be a small matter for a Rockefeller, but not for a colonel. Yet the name Nesbitt had a familiar ring, a connotation of money. What was it? She couldn't remember right now. But one thing she was sure of: Nesbitt's extravagance had other implications. Bribing her professionally with luxury.... Setting up a gorgeous love nest for a mistress? Mike Nesbitt certainly took a lot for granted. It was flattering in a way, but in another, positively insulting, if he thought she was going to fall right into bed with him.

This was just the sort of disillusionment she wanted to shield Charlie from. All of a sudden the beauty, the excitement, of their first meeting, with its connection to the starry spaces, was marred by Lisa's cynical suspicions, and it hurt.

It was not a subject to dwell on now, she reminded herself. There was just too damned much to do. She'd put the hotel matter on hold for the moment. Before she could get back to work, Dieter Heinz came in.

The rest of the day, like the one before, went by like greased lightning. At eleven she was shown into a private office and spent a short time getting it set up and acquainting herself with the trim, efficient woman sergeant, qualified as a medical secretary, who had been assigned to her. She then conferred with Heinz, learning that he'd devised some new tests of his own, much more thorough than the conventional ones. He wanted Lisa's opinion, and she gave it at once. They were intricate, time-consuming and experimental. They were also brilliant and might do the trick. It wasn't likely, though, that in using the new method they'd be able to properly test more than one man a week.

"It'll be faster," Heinz assured her, "as we go along, when we get into the swing of things. The holiday will slow us down, of course. I'd like to schedule Nesbitt tomorrow or Thursday, if that's not too soon."

"Of course." She answered with all the calm she could muster, hoping her face wasn't giving her away.

"As well as being the mission commander, he's the most evasive and the most arrogant of the lot. Therefore, naturally, the most interesting." The old man's eyes twinkled. "I suppose it's to be expected, though, with his background."

"Which part of his background do you mean? I saw a psychological profile on him in New York, but I haven't read all of your report yet." In New York she'd been so intent on his psychological profile that she'd skipped his life history. Except for one fact—his Arien birth date, she thought, repressing a smile, recalling almost with astonishment now how she'd done such a romantic, uncharacteristic thing.

"Why, you know who he *is*, don't you?" Heinz regarded her with some surprise. "Heir to Nesbitt International."

"Good heavens." Of course. That was why his name had seemed so familiar in a financial context—Nesbitt International was an absolute empire, with far-flung and diversified interests that centered around hotels and real estate. Lisa was generally so vague about such things that she hardly paid any attention to them, but now she remembered Greg saying something about Nesbitt stock at some time or other. Mike Nesbitt might *own* the Golden Seasons, for all she knew.

"Lisa?" Heinz was studying her with sharp interest. "Don't look so shocked," he chuckled. "This seems to have some particular significance for you."

"Not at all," she said quickly, but she was sure her whole expression must be quite revealing. "It's just such a...surprise," she added with a feeble smile.

"Nesbitt interests me enormously. He's the apparent despair of his family, who, I gather, would like him to occupy a desk in the Pentagon as a safe, earthbound general. But he has chosen to go his own way. Nevertheless the family hubris remains and shows itself in fascinating ways. Not that he's the only astronaut with a grudge against psychiatry." Heinz chuckled again. "All of them complain about the physical tests, but they seem absolutely hostile to the mental checks. Did you ever meet one who was otherwise?"

"Never. Only me." Lisa grinned, regaining some of her poise and thankful for that. "But that's not exactly the same thing."

"Hardly. I can think of no one whose second opinion...and collaboration...could offend me less."

She broke into laughter at that, because he wore a very mischievous expression. "I'm glad, Dieter."

"You are uniquely qualified, with your background, Lisa, and I think you will be invaluable in helping to solve this problem. You must have guessed it was I who put the bug in Nesbitt's ear about hiring you."

"Well...I really hadn't. I guess that's dense of me," she admitted. So *Heinz* had wanted her, not Mike Nesbitt.

"I must warn you to watch that unpleasant Major Rayburn. He was totally opposed to the expansion of the psychological end of this. He dismissed it as an 'outrageous waste of money.' And, although his military rank is not that high, he does carry weight with the program because of his flight record and his efficiency as an administrator. I think Rayburn may dislike you as much as he does me."

"You've got that right," Lisa said fervently. She told Heinz about her earlier clashes with Rayburn, during her training.

"Ah, the major would relegate all women to 'church, kitchen and nursery,'" Heinz commented, using the well-known German phrase. "Well," he sighed, "we have gossiped enough. Let's get back to our scheduling. I, for one, am looking forward to the Fourth of July. I am not the eager otter I once was...."

She giggled. "Eager *beaver*," she corrected.

"Yes, eager beaver. Thank you." He handed her a copy of the schedules.

Trying to concentrate on them, Lisa was thinking about the Fourth of July. A whole new problem. The way she was feeling now, she'd like to work right through it, but apparently even the hardworking center was going to observe this holiday. Charlie was used to Lisa's ignoring such festivities—some of her patients suffered special anxieties when holidays rolled around, and Lisa had frequently given them emergency counseling on Memorial Day and Labor Day and Christmas. But Lisa could hardly work on the Fourth and leave Charlie to her own devices in a strange city, without her usual friends and places to go.

"The holiday won't harm *you*, Lisa," Heinz remarked suddenly. "You look quite tired. Slow down, my dear child. We don't have to do everything this week, you know."

She murmured in agreement, a bit uncomfortable under the scrutiny of his wise old eyes. After he'd gone back to his office she digested the new information about Mike Nesbitt. His background certainly made a lot of things clear—his casual attitude toward the VIP jet, the palatial hotel, but even more important, his assured, almost arrogant manner, his calm acceptance of eventual victory. He must have been reared with the notion that he could buy anything he wanted...even Lisa Heron and her scientific conclusions.

That idea made her blood boil. It fit right in with her preconceived picture of the superrich. Well, Colonel Nesbitt was in for quite a surprise, she decided.

Then she recalled that she was going to have to test him, interview him, and she was filled with consternation. How could she be objective enough, when he aroused such emotional turmoil? First confusion and desire. Now this disproportionate hostility. There was no way on earth she could get around it. There was only one reason why a psychiatrist could refuse to deal with a client: emotional involvement. She could hardly admit that to Dieter Heinz.

What was worse, she couldn't even vouch for her own feelings right now.... Going on forty, and she wasn't sure. It was revolting. Going on *fourteen* was more like it.

The buzz of her phone startled her. She picked up the intercom. "Colonel Nesbitt, on one."

Great, she thought sarcastically. Nevertheless she answered coolly, "Dr. Heron."

"Lisa?"

That familiar and exciting voice set her pulses racing. But even the one questioning word was spoken blandly; he was obviously still feeling distant. She would take her cue from him, then. With a perverse stubbornness she waited for him to go on.

"Sorry I've been so invisible," he said with more warmth, "but I've really been snowed under. Working with the engineers all hours. I should have called you before. About Thursday."

"Thursday?" she repeated.

"You remember...I'd mentioned taking you and Charlie out to my...to my buddy's ranch."

That slip of the tongue would have puzzled her before; now she understood it. So he owned the ranch, too.

"Are you sure that's convenient?" she asked with cool politeness. "I wouldn't want to trouble you, right in the middle of the project."

"Of *course* it's convenient." He sounded a bit impatient, and that riled her anew. "I thought you and Charlie might want to get out of town for the holiday. My...friends would like to have her...or both of you, of course," he amended hastily, "for the weekend. However, you and I have that conference Friday, you know, before the early closing."

Well, well. So he'd decided to keep pursuing her...and this *was* a ploy to get rid of Charlie for the weekend.

"Yes, of course I was aware of the conference. And as a matter of fact, I was planning on coming in Saturday. So, I really think..."

"But surely it's a good plan for your daughter," he insisted. "Naturally I want you to check it all out first. That's why I'd like you to meet everyone Thursday."

She hesitated. "All right. Thursday, then."

"Great! I'll pick you both up at the hotel about six. The ranch is in the other direction."

Lisa thanked him with grudging civility.

All through the afternoon she was preoccupied with the conversation. She was still convinced that this was part of bigger maneuvers. And yet that night, when she came across the romantic star-novel that she'd absentmindedly brought along, and began to read it again, many of the emotions of those early days inevitably assailed her.

By Wednesday morning she was in a state of utter confusion again. When Nesbitt appeared for his interview and testing, she was newly aware of his overwhelming attractions, but she contrived to keep cool, impressed in spite of herself by his sober, almost respectful manner. There was none of the indulgence in his attitude that women psychiatrists so often met in the skeptical, horseplay-prone astronauts. They often devised elaborate pranks to annoy the psychiatrists, inventing outrageous pictures for the blank-paper drawing test, or boning up on "normal," computer-like answers to psychiatrists' questions, which invalidated the tests.

Lisa had hardly expected that—this was a very serious situation, critical to Nesbitt—but she hadn't foreseen his courtesy to Heinz, or the painful honesty with which he answered certain questions, even volunteering emotion-loaded information. Nesbitt revealed some striking attitudes about the parent-child relationship and again showed uneasiness toward questions of personal commitment, demonstrating a tinge of bitterness.

Considering her own emotional involvement it went better than she'd hoped. But she decided to wait a day to do the evaluation; maybe time would restore some of her objectivity. Mike Nesbitt definitely upset her sensitive equilibrium.

Wednesday evening Lisa was glad to have the distraction of shopping with Charlie for a few items of western gear. She herself had plenty of things left over from three years before. She was absurdly pleased at how well they still fit.

Another pleasant distraction was a long phone call to her father, which Lisa conscientiously charged to her home phone. Phil Marley sounded more like himself than he had in years; and she was heartened. She'd already written him about the technical aspects of the project. Now he said with lively enthusiasm, "You've given me an idea, honey. I'm going to put it together and write you tonight."

Lisa hung up absolutely glowing. That night she slept well, so by the next morning she was much more in command of her thoughts and emotions. She attacked the evaluation of Nesbitt with utter self-confidence, delighted that he had become just an interesting subject, not someone she knew personally...not that disturbing sexual adversary of their first acquaintance.

Having been informed of Nesbitt's invitation to stay at the ranch for the long weekend, Charlie insisted on packing a big canvas bag, although Lisa protested mildly that she might be jumping the gun, that she might not like it that much. But Charlie ridiculed the notion, saying that it would be just like TV and she wasn't going to miss it. Seeing how excited she was, Lisa gave in.

And in spite of all the tangles in the situation, she began to feel a certain excitement herself. This was like their VIP flight to Houston, their first elaborate night.

When they went down to meet Nesbitt in the lobby, Lisa hardly recognized him. He was dressed like a cowhand in faded jeans, a checked shirt and a battered light brown Stetson, which he swept off at once when he sighted them. He strode toward them, smiling, and Lisa was jolted by still another new, attractive image—he might have tethered his horse outside, she thought, he looked so natural this way.

The pale shirt turned his face and neck and arms almost mahogany, and the tight fit of the worn jeans narrowed his hips even more, and made still less of his lean middle. Her glance flicked down to his fine, old boots; he was very easy in them.

"Hidy," Nesbitt drawled, giving "howdy" its full Houston value. "You ladies look as pretty as pictures and as cool as clear water."

His grin widened, and Lisa got the feeling he was mocking his own movie-cowboy image for their benefit. He was so many different men, she thought, delighted with the whole evening all of a sudden.

Charlie was thrilled. "There *are* real cowboys in Houston!"

"Not me, Charlie." He still spoke in a teasing voice, but he sounded more like himself now. "Shall we?"

He opened the doors to the Mercedes with a flourish, and soon they were heading out of town on the Southwest Freeway toward the open country.

"Where's the desert?" Charlie demanded, leaning forward with great interest.

"Farther west," Nesbitt explained. "And to the northwest, in the Panhandle. Actually, this is a lot like some of the coastal areas of Florida, where I come from."

Lisa thought so, too, seeing more green and trees than she had expected; she wasn't too familiar with this territory.

"What are those things?" Charlie queried.

"Oil pumps. We won't be seeing desert, but just about everywhere you go in Texas you'll see oil," Nesbitt replied.

His easy, amiable manner, his readiness to answer Charlie's constant questions, were enough to put Lisa at her ease. But sitting so close to him, she was discovering as the miles unwound behind them, discomfited her all over again, though at the same time it thrilled her in every nerve.

Only half listening to Charlie's eager words and Nesbitt's good-natured answers, Lisa reacted more to the timbre of his voice than to what he said. The first days of their acquaintance, with all their unreal loveliness, were vivid in her mind once more. She was sharply conscious of his big, lean body next to her; the massive hands in command of the wheel; the long muscular legs straining against the tight denim of his faded jeans, his booted feet.

She didn't dare turn to look at his profile; her eyes would give too much away. It was incredible how many of her doubts—and how much of her logic—were canceled out in his physical presence.

"We've just passed through the metropolis of Lariat, population eighty-seven. The biggest town in Texas," Lisa heard him say with a chuckle.

Charlie grinned. "Mike, what's—"

Lisa broke in with mild reproof. "The quiz show's over for the moment, kiddo." She'd noticed that Nesbitt's voice was sounding a bit strained, his travelogue somewhat artificial.

"Let's just *look* a while," Lisa suggested gently.

"I read you."

Lisa turned and grinned at Charlie to soften her reproof; then she glanced aside at Mike Nesbitt. His swift glance back, his half smile, said a wry thanks.

They drove on in peaceful quiet for a time, and Lisa watched the magnificent Texas sunset fill the sky. There was an aura created by the very vastness of the country; a noticeable blueness prevailed just before the sun was gone. In the comparative emptiness the sky was absolutely filled with sunset, unlike the fragmented views the tall buildings in the crowded city allowed.

Lisa drew in her breath, positively dazzled. She heard Charlie saying, "Ohhh...it's so *beautiful.*"

Glancing again at Nesbitt, she saw him nod. "A sunset isn't just a sunset in Texas," he said. "Every day it's an event."

Then the sun was gone, and his next announcement, matter-of-fact and plain, shattered the spell of the moment and reminded her of rude reality and all the difficulties that still lay between them.

"We'll be there in a few minutes. This is the turnoff."

He turned off the highway and drove more slowly down a winding, tree-lined road. Another turn and they were entering a long driveway, through a metal gate surmounted by a single star and a sign reading "Houstar" that led to a sprawling white house. It was nearly twilight, and the house was brilliantly lit. Lisa saw a patio and the glimmer of a swimming pool to the left. A tall old man in western gear, and a plump, smiling woman in a severe, chic cotton dress, were standing on the patio, smiling and waving.

Mike braked on a grassy oval and got out, calling, "Hidy, Martha...Frank, how you doing?" He opened the passenger door and held out his hand to Lisa. When she put her hand in his she felt that same disconcerting electric shock she'd felt the first day in her office in New York. His grip tightened for a second.

But Lisa released her hand quickly. Charlie opened her own door and got out; then there was a flurry of greetings and introductions. Nesbitt was embracing Martha, pumping her husband's hand, presenting them to Lisa as the Harrises.

"My goodness—" Martha Harris twinkled at Lisa and Charlie "—you didn't tell me you were bringing *movie* stars!"

Charlie beamed, and Lisa glowed at the compliment. If anyone else had said it, it would have sounded phony, but she had the strangest feeling that Martha Harris sincerely meant it, that there wasn't a phony bone in the woman's body. She looked like someone who was secure and happy in herself, with a nature that was open and generous.

"You're very sweet," Lisa said, and impulsively kissed Martha on the cheek.

When they were going in the front door, Nesbitt asked, "Where are the boys?"

Frank Harris said, "They're gettin' all gussied up for company. They were a little late coming in this evening." Lisa liked the looks of the man; he was weathered, grizzled and wiry, reminding her of one of her favorite character actors. And though he seemed to be the soul of good nature, his deep gray eyes were sharp and observant. He had the look of a competent, intelligent man.

The entrance hall was beautiful. Martha, after asking if Lisa and Charlie wanted to freshen up, and receiving their disclaimer, led the way into an even lovelier living room furnished in the traditional manner. It might, Lisa decided, have been a fine suburban living room anywhere; there were very few western touches.

While they were being served cocktails, two tall young men came downstairs and ambled through the archway into the room. One, introduced as Tony, was a younger version of Frank; Tony's hair was pitch black, and his gray eyes were striking against his deep tan. The other, George, was heavier and shorter than his brother; his face had the amiable fullness of Martha's, and his eyes, like hers, were dark. But both of them looked equally tough and able.

While they were getting their own drinks, the sons regarded Lisa with respectful admiration, but were apparently flabbergasted by Charlie. As the others talked about the ranch and the space program, Lisa covertly watched George and Tony flirting with her delighted daughter.

In spite of all her other concerns, particularly her ambivalent feelings for Nesbitt, Lisa felt a warm sense of well-being steal over her.

It persisted throughout dinner, which was served at a long, shining table in the elegant dining room, and afterward on the patio, where they sat talking.

"How about a swim, Charlie?" Tony drawled. "Did you bring a suit? If you didn't, we've got plenty of extras around here."

Before Charlie could answer, Frank Harris said, "Plenty of time for that tomorrow, boy. You *are* staying, aren't you, Miss Charlie? How 'bout it, Dr. Heron?"

"Look, I don't want Charlie to wear out her welcome..." Lisa began.

"But we're *planning* on it!" Martha exclaimed, and the loud protests of Frank Harris and the boys nearly drowned out Martha.

"I'd *love* to, Ma." That seemed to settle it.

Then Charlie was telling them she'd brought plenty of things, Lisa was saying something to Martha about her strong-minded daughter, and Tony was rushing to the Mercedes to get Charlie's bag. There was a whole new flurry. Martha directed Tony to put the bag in the pink room, and finally Mike and Lisa were saying good night, explaining that they had work in Houston tomorrow, but would probably be coming back on Saturday or Sunday, depending on how things went.

Lisa's heart fluttered; she wondered just what he meant by that, then concluded that it referred to work. After all, she had told him that she'd be going in on Saturday.

Soon they were waving goodbye, heading down the long driveway to the winding road, and turning onto the highway again for the drive back to Houston.

"I like your friends," Lisa said. "It's so sweet of them to invite Charlie to stay." She waited for him to tell her that Houstar was his ranch, that he'd arranged it all himself.

But he didn't. "They're nice people," he agreed. "We've been...friends for a long, long time. If Martha were older, she'd be like a kind of mother to me, I guess."

Lisa experienced a sudden, disturbing unease. Why was he being so secretive with her? Why did he think it mattered who owned the ranch? For some reason she recalled certain aspects of his tests that had puzzled her—a hint of coldness when he was questioned about his mother, and that same evasive tone, that resistance to personal commitment, that she'd found in the New York records.

She was so preoccupied that they covered long miles in silence. They were almost in Houston before he asked tentatively, "Would you like a nightcap before I take you home?"

Lisa paused for an instant, then said, "Yes. I would." She told herself that she wanted to talk to him about the project, but even as she did so she realized that was a pretty lame excuse. She simply wanted to be with him a little longer; she was teased and challenged by the way he'd reverted with such apparent ease to the role of host. With every hour they'd spent together tonight, she'd found herself warming to him more.

He looked extremely pleased with her acceptance. They were in the city now, and he asked, "Want to try an ice house?"

"What on earth is that?" she demanded. "I must have missed it before."

He laughed. "You'll see. Okay?"

"Why not? In this weather an ice house sounds fine." She noticed that they were near Rice University.

"Here we are." She saw some open garage doors, and picnic tables scattered around a grassy spot. Nearby some men were pitching horseshoes.

When they got out, she heard, incredibly, the sound of chamber music. "I don't believe this," she said, laughing. "It's...unique."

"Only in Houston," he assured her, taking her lightly by the elbow, leading her to one of the picnic tables. "You can have Bach with your beer, Vivaldi with your vino."

He pulled out a bench, and they sat down close together. A queer, abrupt flutter sounded in Lisa's ears. Her skin felt hot, and her breath quickened. She thought, I shouldn't have come here with him.

Then, perversely, she was almost annoyed that he didn't seem as affected as she was. He was chatting easily, telling her about the ice houses, and she forced herself to listen.

"This place dates back to the days when folks used to come to buy big blocks of ice, and the fellow who ran it would keep a few bottles of beer for his customers. Then refrigerators came along, and...no more ice houses." He smiled down at her, and she was more aware than ever of his stunning attractiveness. The impulsive, generous mouth that had tasted so exciting, had aroused such fire when he had kissed her, might never have touched her own, he seemed so distant and casual. And she couldn't read the expression in his vivid eyes.

"Except this kind of ice house," he concluded lightly, and asked her what she'd like to drink.

He ordered wine for her and a beer for himself. She moved slightly away from him, feeling self-conscious and doubtful, wondering what he was up to, why he had suddenly become so formal.

She struggled to start another conversation, but finally gave up and fell silent, looking around her, listening to the music. For one wild moment she decided she must be dreaming. Could she actually be sitting on a picnic bench in Texas with an astronaut and listening to Vivaldi? An astronaut who had tried to make love to her the first day they met, swept her off to Houston, made passionate overtures to her again, then backed off abruptly...and suddenly switched back again to distant friendliness...a man who had seemed so open, but who was really a very secretive person, hiding his deepest feelings, and even the fact that he must be a very rich man.

And a man who shared her passion for the exploration of unknown space. Lisa looked up at the twinkling stars above them, amazed at how visible they were, free of the smog of the cities she had known.

Now she had a feeling he was staring at her. She looked at him. He had a strange smile on his mouth, and an even stranger secretiveness in his eyes.

A swift, dismaying idea occurred to her: was the pogo in the equipment, or in Mike Nesbitt? But no, that was absurd. It had also affected his men, and...

She was getting a headache, and now the pleasant night was full of new uncertainty and discomfort.

She said casually, "The stars are so bright over Texas." He stared at her, not answering her smile, and she added, "I like your ice house, but I think it's getting late. And I've got to be in early tomorrow."

Lisa questioned her own perversity again when he concurred, asking for the bill and paying it quickly.

When they were back in the car, heading for the hotel, she thought, as she had once before, you're the one with pogo, Lisa Heron. If he tries to make love to you, you stop him; if he doesn't, you're annoyed.

After Nesbitt dropped her at the hotel with a good-night that was merely friendly, Lisa went to her suite feeling more indecisive than ever.

Trying to get to sleep, she reflected that maybe Charlie was right and a lot of it could be chalked up to astrology—she recalled what Charlie had told her about Aries people. They rushed in with enormous enthusiasm, then just as quickly changed their minds. Maybe Nesbitt's early feelings for her had changed, and now he was only living up to polite commitments he'd made when they first arrived in Houston—showing Charlie life on a ranch, for one thing, extending the same invitation to Lisa just because she was Charlie's mother. Perhaps the invitation to have a nightcap had been made only out of politeness; she should have declined.

And yet...and yet, she couldn't quite accept that explanation. She couldn't forget for a moment the way things had been in New York, or the night when he had driven her down to the wharves.

On the other hand, there was the evidence of his rather mysterious psychological profile, indicating a secretive quality that his open manner belied. And there was also the inescapable suspicion that he would try to maneuver her into agreement in the project: Aries people liked to lead, enjoyed the feel of power.

One of the few things she was sure of was that Mike Nesbitt was a headache, literally and figuratively.

There were two more sure things. One, she was going to avoid the weekend at the ranch. Charlie would be fine there.

And number two was that she'd get her mind on business, period. And keep it there.

She woke up the next morning refreshed and confident, more determined than ever to get herself back on course. She was ready well ahead of time, so she sat down with the papers she'd brought to the hotel.

Rereading a copy of her evaluation of Nesbitt, Lisa was pleased with its fair, objective tone. She believed she'd regained her detachment. Skimming through the other evaluations, she decided that it would be safe to present a tentative decision at the meeting this morning: from all the evidence, and despite certain interesting quirks of Nesbitt's, it was obvious to Lisa that the team members who had been interviewed so far were perfectly normal and able men, and that the problem might well be purely technical.

When she went downstairs for breakfast and passed the desk, the man on duty handed her a special-delivery letter. It was from her father. Lisa hurried into the coffee shop—or what passed for a coffee shop in that golden palace—sat down and eagerly tore open the envelope.

She was so intent on the letter that she hardly knew what she ordered, or when her breakfast was put before her. Phil Marley's theories, as set forth in his detailed letter, confirmed what she had concluded.

Lisa smiled. He'd written, "You're the doctor, but I'm still the engineer." And he'd gone on to offer a brilliant suggestion. She couldn't wait to show it to Nesbitt and the engineering staff. This was wonderful.

Even more wonderful was the fact that her father was as inventive and able as ever. Somehow that was more important than all the projects in the world. Lisa no longer had any patience with breakfast; she drank a cup of coffee, nibbled at the toast and decided to call her father at once.

But when she reached the lobby she realized it was still far too early in New York; she'd call him at lunchtime. Meanwhile the letter had absolutely made her day, and she rushed to the copter site feeling that all the reins were in her hands again.

The elation lasted throughout the brief flight and her early conference with Heinz. At the staff meeting everything began to fall apart.

She'd decided to hold off on presenting her father's theory until she'd had a chance to confer with the engineers. If she jumped to conclusions too fast, the hostile Rayburn and his allies would be sure to use it against her to try to discredit her judgment.

Therefore she and Heinz confined themselves to a cautious evaluation, referring merely to an "apparent trend."

As Lisa had expected, Rayburn reacted very contentiously to that, and the proceedings became more and more unpleasant as the meeting wore on.

She was dismayed to find that she had another problem: Mike Nesbitt. As soon as he walked into the conference room she found her concentration scattering.

All her optimism and self-confidence disappeared. She'd never seen him look more impressive or magnetic or...utterly remote. None of her firm resolves of the night before or this morning seemed to help, and she found that she was letting Heinz carry the main burden of the presentation.

Nesbitt did react strongly in opposition to Rayburn, but that, she concluded with gloom, was nothing new. They'd obviously been adversaries for a long time, and Nesbitt would naturally support anyone who implied that the problem was technical, not medical.

Why am I even thinking like this, she questioned in miserable silence. She should be concentrating on the job, not on this maddening, attractive man. This unforeseen crumbling of her defenses upset her no end.

She managed to get through the rest of the meeting, though, with enough poise to save face. At the end of it, she walked away quickly with Heinz to avoid having to talk with Nesbitt.

Then she excused herself to Heinz, telling him that she'd have a sandwich at her desk, and fled to her office, where she shut the door. She asked the sergeant to order her some lunch, then put through a call to her father on Long Island.

While she waited for the connection, she thought unhappily about how different this was from what she'd anticipated that morning. Nevertheless she summoned up all her enthusiasm and told herself that she'd done very well. When her call went through she forced that enthusiasm into her voice, and by the time she hung up her father sounded buoyant. She promised to keep in touch with him as often as possible. Meanwhile the engineering staff was scattering for the weekend, and it might not be possible for her to see all of them together until Tuesday morning.

Annoyed all over again with the interruptive holiday, Lisa decided to check in with Charlie. Martha answered the phone, saying that Charlie was in the pool and they were all having a marvelous time; then she asked Lisa when she'd join them.

Lisa made an evasive answer, told Martha not to bother Charlie right then, and hung up.

She didn't do much better with lunch than she'd done with breakfast; her mind was in such turmoil that the food tasted like sawdust. But she forced her sandwich down, not wanting to arouse the curiosity of the motherly sergeant, then wished her aide a happy weekend when the time came for early closing.

Listening to the other offices empty out, Lisa thought, I'm just spinning my wheels. What a frustrating weekend it was going to be—she'd either be doing the social number, which she was in no mood for even with Charlie and the Harrises, or she'd be moping alone in the hotel, too preoccupied with the project to think of anything else.

Alone.

Now why did that stand out like a sore thumb? Because all of a sudden she was extremely lonely. Even Greg would have been a welcome companion; she felt almost nostalgic about him, and *very* nostalgic about New York. Generally on the Fourth of July Charlie went out to Long Island to visit her grandmother, whose neighbors had a lot of teenage children, or to the Cape.

Lisa and Greg generally stayed in town, catching up on work during the day and in the evening going to an air-conditioned restaurant, concert or play.

Manhattan was so beautifully empty on holidays, Lisa thought. Greg always said, "This is when the *real* New Yorkers inherit...we diehards." Maybe she shouldn't have been so flip in her goodbye to him, so blasé in their dealings. He was a marvelous companion. Never maddening.

Like Michael Nesbitt, Lieutenant Blasted Colonel.

She heard a man's footfall in the quiet corridor, then a quick, soft tapping at her door. She called out "Come in," then saw that her visitor was Mike Nesbitt.

His vivid blue eyes had such a fierce, almost angry expression that she asked, "What is it...? What's the matter? Have there been some new developments?"

Unsmiling, he stood at the door. "No, nothing new. The same old trouble."

"What do you mean? If you're talking about the conference this morning..."

He was staring at her hard, and his eyes changed. A whole new expression struggled with the fierce anger. "Not the conference, Lisa. *You're* my problem."

Lisa's heart began to pound. She couldn't say a single word.

Chapter 5

Lisa watched him move toward her, and she was struck once again with that sense of fatefulness, of inevitability, that she had known in New York at their first encounter.

And then she realized, with a kind of parenthetical vanity, that she was still wearing her big owlish glasses.

For the first time a little smile lightened his face. When he reached her he leaned over, took the glasses off and said quietly, "I'm talking about the thing we've been avoiding."

He came around the desk and stood beside her. Then he was bending over, twirling her around in her chair to face him, urging her to stand with the pressure of his fingers that, meeting hers again, were as charged as they'd been on that first amazing day. She felt an instant shock, a crackle of electricity along her nerves.

Dazed, she stood. He grabbed her in arms that bound her like steel. In her astonished memory the lines from *Hamlet* sang: Those friends thou hast, and their adoption tried, Grapple them to thy soul with hoops of steel....

Nesbitt's "adoption" certainly hadn't been tried, yet already she felt like that about him. Then she couldn't think at all. He was holding her nearer, making a hungry, pleading sound and covering her surprised mouth with his. Lisa felt her blood dissolve into swirling fire, and the sound in her ears was like the roar of a rocket zooming from its gantry. She was no longer conscious of anything in the universe except that she was bound in the circle of his potent arms.

She was somewhere beyond measurable time, in a place where the hours were calculated only in light. All she was sure of was that it would be agony to let him go. It didn't matter now where they were, or who, or what else happened. She returned his wild caress with all her heart, knowing that each long year of loneliness was in her savage fervor.

At last, when their lips were slightly apart, he said her name with a gasping, ragged breath, and she heard herself protesting languidly, from far away, "Oh, Mike. Mike. Not here. Not here."

His drunken-looking gaze seemed to clear a little, and he murmured, "No. No, not here."

Neither seemed to notice or care now that nothing else was said; nothing else needed to be said, for the moment. Everything was settled.

Like a sleepwalker she gathered up her bag, letting her papers lie as they were. She glanced in the mirror on the wall as she passed it, dimly aware that her face was all right, but that her eyes were huge and glazed, as if she were hypnotized.

He opened the door and waited for her to step into the empty hall; then they walked down the echoing white corridor past locked doors and deserted offices. She blinked in the brilliant redness of the sunset behind the parking space and got into the Mercedes as if her whole body were on automatic.

There were a few random employees also leaving late. Nesbitt caught her eyes, telling her silently that he wanted to kiss her again now, when he couldn't; then they were pulling away, and he was driving toward Houston. They still hadn't exchanged another word.

She realized incredibly soon that they were pulling up in front of the Golden Seasons. Nesbitt surrendered the car to a smiling, smart attendant and then walked through the lobby. She felt as if she were floating in space; her legs were weak and rubbery and strange, and the ascent in the elevator, in which they were alone, passed like a brief dream interval.

At last they were inside the suite. The final rays of sunset had turned the gold and creamy furnishings a brilliant orange-rose, and she had a swift, lovely thought that it looked more like sunrise than the end of day.

He smiled at her and strode to the wide windows, where he drew the pale golden draperies. Now everything in the room was tinged with gold.

She was overcome with delight when he said, in harmony with her impression, "Golden Lisa...you look all gold." He stared at her for a moment, seeming to devour her with his eyes, and then he was beside her again, taking her close, with one hand stroking her cheek and neck and hair, and murmuring, "You're the loveliest woman I've ever known, the loveliest thing in all my life."

Melted by his words, his look and her own newly raging need, she pressed her body to his, learning all its wondrous hardness, grasping his head with her hands, kneading his hair with her trembling fingers. Then her hands slid down the sides of his head, feeling the leaping pulse beneath his skin as he cried out again and covered her mouth with his once more.

While his hard hands explored her arms and shoulders, traced her breasts and moved shakily to her waist and slender hips, her aroused flesh shuddered with even greater desire, and her own hands felt hungrily for his shoulders, then wandered down over his chest and stole inside his khaki shirt. She began to unbutton the buttons. His skin felt as if it were on fire.

He raised his mouth from hers, whispering, "Lisa, Lisa," and then he was kissing her neck. She could feel the tip of his tongue. Her skin pulsated; her whole being throbbed, and she cried out.

With gentle haste he removed her jacket, unfastened the buttons on the front of her dress. The dress slid down around her feet, and she sensed the cooling touch of the air on her feverish skin. She felt so weak now that she could barely stand. He stepped back and surveyed her lightly tanned body in its frail coverings of golden lace.

He undid her thin brassiere and, letting it fall, bent down to explore her trembling breasts with his ardent mouth, all the while stroking her sides, her hips, with his excited fingers, until she felt a wildness of desire so intense she raged and shuddered with it. He peeled away her bikini of flowered lace, kneeling before her to grasp one ankle, then another, signaling her to let him slip her sandals from her bare feet.

All of her was known to him now. He looked up, slowly, worshipfully, from her feet to her desirous face, and murmured, "Golden lady, golden Lisa."

Keeping his hands on her, he stood and captured her with one hard arm. She could sense a throbbing in his tensed muscles that spoke of a need so great it must have been excruciating. Close together, they walked toward her bedroom. On the threshold he lifted her into his arms, kissing her with barbaric abandon on her brows, cheeks and eyelids, ultimately finding her trembling, parted mouth.

The pressure of that starved, hot kiss, the friction of his tough skin on the softness of her naked body, titillated her to a new astonishment of wanting; she felt as if her flesh were being brushed with flames. He placed her in the center of the bed.

Waiting, vibrant, she watched through the filter of her half-shut lashes the final baring of his splendid torso, then his narrow haunches and his long, tanned, powerful legs. The hair on his body was red gold in contrast to the darkness of his skin. The lighter patch of skin around his loins, where his bathing trunks had shadowed him from the sun, was startling and provocative, tickling her to even greater yearning, lending a seductive emphasis to his strong arousal.

She raised her wondering look to his face; his eyes had never been so dazzling. And, denuded of its genial mockery, his expressive mouth was tender, vulnerable with his overpowering need.

"Oh..." she murmured, and he came to her slowly, marveling at the sight of her. He lowered himself to her with the *adagio* motion of an awestruck visitor from an alien world, adapting his limbs and weight to the dreamlike pull of a foreign gravity.

Now they were close, so close, wound in each other's arms, and he was caressing her gently again with his hands and his lips, until guided by her knowledge of his painful need, she drew him to her and their bodies wholly blended. He made a sound of ineffable wonder. The deep sigh of his first release was resonant in her ears, and with an even greater pleasure than before she welcomed the return of her own desire, and gave herself up to it, meeting him, joining him in that final release. Their outcries melded. She experienced, with a fullness and profundity that she could never have imagined, the ultimate wonder. The shattering, piercing mystery left its lingering ripples over all her skin, and left them both in breathless silence.

They were lying close again in their dazzled quiet; his big hand kneaded her head, stroking her fine, tumbled hair. Finally he raised her chin to study her face; the vivid blue eyes were indescribably tender in their drowsiness. He kissed her delicately on her eyebrow, then her nose, afterward leaning down to kiss her softened mouth.

"Lisa, my golden Lisa," he whispered. "This is like...the centrifuge. I feel all...light and heavy, all at once."

"So do I, darling. So do I." She kissed his neck. He made a sound of growling contentment and settled her more comfortably against his wide, hair-roughened chest. She rubbed her head against him and felt his arm tighten around her.

After a moment of stillness, while she listened to the slowing beat of his excited heart, he murmured, "There's so much I want to say to you." She lay there without an answer, simply enjoying the resonance of his voice against her cheek, like a muted trumpet.

"Darling?" he prompted gently.

She told him what she'd been thinking, and looked up to see his smile. He kissed her again, briefly, and his smile grew broader. "That book again. I'm glad you read about our starry friends. I have a feeling it helped get us here...now."

"Perhaps it did." She grinned and laid her head back on his chest, aware that the miracle of their closeness had broken their dam of silence.

Now he began to let loose a flood of confiding words. "Lisa, I want to tell you what it's been like for me...maybe explain some of the things that seemed unexplainable. Make you understand why at times I've been acting like a Grade-A...juvenile...jackass."

She smiled so broadly that she knew he could feel the smile against him, but as he went on she sobered. He was so very earnest that she felt tenderness move like a sunbeam over her body.

"I knew that very first minute," he was saying, "when I saw you on the terrace in New York, that I had never wanted a woman so much or so fast in all my life. Then, when I found out who you were, how complicated it might be, I was stymied for a second."

A *second,* she repeated in amused silence. Aries people *are* swift, she reflected. But she kept her peace; he was being so utterly open that she didn't have the heart, or the desire, to tease him.

But he read her all the same, because he laughed at himself. "Yes, a second. That was long enough. I decided then and there, in your office, that getting you to Houston was my first priority...I must admit, I was as anxious to get you for an associate as I was eager to get to...know you."

"In the biblical sense, that is," she retorted.

"Absolutely. Anyway, I couldn't get you out of my mind the whole afternoon—I just roamed around the Village, a little high on you, working out practical details...just in case. And then, as I told you, I got into my courting gear and waited for you in Washington Square Park, and followed you to that restaurant. Then, after I...got out of control and grabbed you at your door, I was really afraid. Afraid that I'd blown it for good—all of it. Besides wanting you so much I couldn't see straight, I did need you—*do* need you—for the project."

"I have a confession to make," she said, raising her face from his chest and looking him in the eyes. "I thought that you might be capable of...well, seducing me into agreeing with your conclusions."

He was flabbergasted. "You thought *that?*" His hand trailed along her face almost absently as he dealt with his surprise. "That never even occurred to me...well, not with someone like you."

In an abashed way, he confessed that he *had* thought about sweet-talking her—until he'd met her. Then he put his arm around her again.

"But not you. You're far too bright to be manipulated...too beautiful, and too sassy, to fall for anything like that. You really amaze me. I've never been much of a lady-killer." He twinkled at her. Her suspicions seemed to have perversely pleased him.

"You nearly killed this one, Colonel," she retorted, only half joking. "I've been in a state of utter confusion ever since we met. You were so cool that first day at the center. And, appropriately enough," she quipped, "at the ice house."

He caressed her vibrant body. "That first day at the center I was hurting from the night before; at the ice house I was trying my damnedest to be good. And I'm here to tell you it wasn't easy. It's never easy to be around you and not touch you, kiss you." They were silent again, enjoying each other's nearness. "I sweated blood," he said, "until you okayed Houston, Lisa. I admit I was hoping for a trip for two—look, don't misunderstand me. Charlie's a great kid."

"That occurred to me, too, Mike," she admitted. "Which brings me to confession number two." All of a sudden it was vital to her to be as open with him as he was being with her.

"To wit...?" He was playing with the fall of hair around her ear. She reacted at once to the affectionate touch.

"I thought the ranch trip," she said slowly, "might be a ploy to dispose of my daughter."

"Well, it was...partly. Are you going to court-martial me for that, ma'am?" His tone was light, but his eyes were serious.

"No, Colonel. Not for a moment. As it turns out, it's a convenient arrangement...isn't it?" She hugged him, wanting to express her understanding. "This is *our* time.... We're entitled to it."

"Damn right," he agreed fervently. "While we're letting it all hang out, I may as well go all the way." He released her, leaned over to retrieve cigarettes and lighter from the pocket of his fallen shirt and, after she'd declined a proffered smoke, lit his. Then he punched his pillow and leaned back again, exhaling with relish. He turned to her. "I haven't been backing off, exactly, these last few days. You can imagine what the engineering labs have been like; we've been sweating over that fault night and day. As a matter of fact, I was planning to get together with you on it Tuesday morning...but enough. This isn't the time or place." His smile was very sweet, she thought.

"Tell me," he said abruptly. "It was tough for you, examining me the other day, wasn't it?"

She nodded. "You knew, then. Yes, one of the toughest things I've ever had to do. Needless to say, my objectivity wasn't at its greatest."

"Neither was my total honesty." He looked at her levelly. "I had some cockamamie idea that I didn't want you, as a woman, to discover any...weaknesses, any pogo in me. Aside from what it means to the project."

He put out his cigarette and continued soberly, "There's still a lot you don't know about me, Lisa. And now that...this has happened—" his fingers squeezed her arm "—I want you to know it all. That business about parents and kids, for instance. First of all, I didn't have a very ordinary childhood. My dad is Nesbitt International."

She nodded. "I know. Heinz told me the other day."

He was studying her. "And you didn't know that before? That first night, and the night on the wharves?"

"No. I never thought of it. Why do you ask?" She was puzzled.

"I'll get to that. But you can't imagine how glad I am about what you just told me." He looked tender, elated. "I had every material advantage in the world as a kid, but the atmosphere in the house was...pretty awful. As soon as my brother and I were born, my mother suddenly didn't give a damn about my father anymore. Naturally that made things tense between us and him.

"It's crazy, but I vowed I'd never have any kids of my own to come between me and my wife, when I got one.... I was going to have someone who'd be all mine, and I'd be all hers. Period. Then a few years ago I met a woman who wasn't what she seemed. I found out that she...was marrying Nesbitt International, not Mike Nesbitt. It knocked me for a loop; I made another vow—that I'd never marry, never try to love a woman again." He paused and studied her as if trying to gauge her reaction.

"So much of it is clear now," she said gently. "Your bitterness about personal commitment, your unusual attitude to the parent-child tie. I understand, Mike...totally. And I'm beginning to understand why you're glad I didn't know you were part of an empire." She caressed his arm, and he reached across and took her hand, holding it tightly.

He chuckled. "I was really touched when you made your protest about the Seasons being, what was it, a little elaborate? My family owns this hotel, Lisa."

She shook her head. "And...Houstar, too, I gather?"

"You're one smart lady. Houstar isn't just a ranch, honey. It's also Houstar Oil." He looked at her mischievously. "You can't imagine, you really can't, what it means to me...learning you didn't know a damn thing about my, shall we say, status in the world, before you let me kiss you that first night, and that wonderful night later, on the pier. But I'm an even bigger fool to be surprised. You're not the kind of woman who *would* think about those things." His eyes admired her.

"I'm not some kind of saint." She grinned. "I think money's perfectly delightful. It's just that it never...played a big role in my life. I think when you're a comfortable, middle-class type you just don't consider it, somehow. All my energies have been directed into...achieving something, making a modest amount of my own money. That's all; nothing noble."

He leaned over and kissed her softly, gently. "You make it sound like nothing, but to me it's a hell of a lot. I guess being valued for...myself means more to me than to other people."

"Then you've got no problem now." She began to tease his arm, his shoulder, then his chest and neck, with light, nibbling kisses, and she could feel him take fire.

"Right at this moment, lady," he muttered against her lips, "there's not a problem in the whole western world."

And then, with soft haste, they were coming together again.

Lisa's first thought as she opened her eyes to darkness was that they must have slept for quite a while. She heard Mike stirring beside her; he reached out his arms and she cuddled up against him.

"Ummm," he growled with drowsy pleasure. "Sleeping like that was so nice." They kissed lightly; then he switched on the lamp by the bed. He reached for his watch. "Nine o'clock...I can't believe it."

She stretched. "We needed it. I think we were both pretty tired."

"You've got that right. It's been quite a week...quite an evening. Listen, Doctor, when was your last meal?"

"A whole one? Last night," she confessed. "Crumbs of breakfast, ditto lunch."

"That's awful! I'm going to order us something right now. What would you like?"

"Order for me. I'm going to shower and slip into something more presentable." She slipped out of bed, feeling ridiculously self-conscious.

He mock-leered at her naked skin. "There *isn't* anything more presentable." She laughed at his villainous accent. "Go, go, your highness, and I'll have the slaves bring us comestibles."

She hurried into the bath and took a hasty shower; then, draped in a towel, she opened the door and went back to the bedroom to dress, choosing a glamorous lounging outfit she'd never worn before.

Mike could be heard murmuring on the phone in the living room. He must be planning something very special. That made her feel happier, more glowing than ever. Her outside looks, she noticed, matched her inner shine. Her eyes were practically starry—I don't think they've looked like that for years, she decided—and her fine pale hair glittered smoothly. Her mouth had ripened.

"Hello, hel-*lo*," he greeted her when she went in the living room. His torso was bare, but he'd slipped on his uniform trousers. "I've been busy with all kinds of orders," he said. "Someone's going to bring up my emergency bag from the car. Don't look like that," he added, laughing at her uncertain expression. "I didn't know *this* was going to happen; I always carry extra clothes for when I have to work overnight at the center. Come here."

She obeyed, and he held her against him, saying with appreciation, "You smell as good as you look." He stood back and held both her hands. "I like that. It's beautiful. *You're* beautiful."

"Thank you, Colonel." Her answer was flip, but her heart was full. She almost felt like crying. She was so happy, feeling so elated.

"Now, excuse me a minute while I shower. If my luck is in, the fresh stuff will be here any minute." He went off to the bath. She heard a rush of water and loud, off-key singing.

She was still grinning when the buzzer sounded. An impassive attendant handed her Nesbitt's canvas bag, and she thanked the man, tipped him and took the bag into the bedroom, calling out, "Your new gear has just been issued, sir."

The water was off and he heard. "I thank you, madam. I'll be with you in two minutes."

He almost made it; she was astonished at his speed. He was wearing an off-white knitted shirt, with well-tailored gray-green slacks. He looked absolutely wonderful, and she told him so.

But in contrast to her feeling of languor and ease, he seemed to be tense, expectant. She began to wonder why, whether it had something to do with dinner, because when the buzzer sounded again he almost raced to the door.

"Let me!" He sounded so excited that she was totally mystified. He murmured something to the waiter, handed him a bill, and after the man had gone, stood with his back to her, doing something to one of the covered dishes.

Then he let out an explosive sigh, as if in relief, and wheeled the cart into the middle of the room.

"Voilá!" he exclaimed. "Approach, *madame*. I suggest you try this dish first."

Still puzzled, but already smiling at the prospect of some special surprise, Lisa went to the table. With a flourish, Mike swept the cover from the largest covered dish. A brown velvet box reposed on the empty chased silver plate.

"What on earth?" she demanded.

"For you. It's been burning a hole in my suitcase since...last Saturday." He handed her the box.

"Last *Saturday*?" She opened the lid and gasped. Arranged on the ivory velvet interior was a glittering display, an Arabian Nights treasure trove: at the top, a pair of diamond earring jackets in the shape of delicate stars; below them, in two dazzling rows, twelve sets of jeweled studs to wear with the jackets.

Incredulous, Lisa murmured, "You should have said 'Open Sesame.'" There were blazing blue-green Australian opals, orange fire opals, a pair of blue-white diamonds; flawless, creamy pearls, and a pair that looked like rare brown diamonds, which she'd only seen pictures of till now.

In addition there were black pearls, golden orange honey topaz, milky opals and rose diamonds. Completing this fantasy array were three other sets—bloodred rubies, dark red garnets and lime-green peridots.

"Mike." She was still too overwhelmed to know quite what to say. He'd bought this last *Saturday,* the day after they'd met. While the impulsiveness and downright craziness of that almost dismayed her—it made him seem utterly reckless, even lacking in judgment—she couldn't help being moved by the gesture. Why, he'd actually chosen the colors that blended with her hair and eyes and wardrobe...chosen stars, which were so significant, and bought twelve pairs of earrings, one for each zodiacal sign. No one in all her life had ever even thought of giving her such imaginative, outrageously extravagant riches.

She hesitated painfully, not sure she could take it. This was like an engagement present. Was she ready for that kind of commitment? But maybe to him it was just a trinket, offered to a woman he admired.

Lisa was aware of the awkward pause and wished she didn't always have to analyze everything so damned much.

"Mike," she said slowly, "this is exquisite. I've never even seen anything like it. But it's so...extravagant..." She was on the point of saying, "that I just can't accept it," when she caught the expression in his eyes. He looked as if he were offering her his heart along with the jewels.

She remembered her mother saying that part of the art of life was learning "gracious acceptance," that some people needed to give gifts so much it was like a hunger.

Echoing the memory, Nesbitt stopped in the act of opening champagne to say, "Please, Lisa. You don't know how long it's been since I've wanted to give someone something special.... You don't realize what a little thing this is compared to what you've given me. And I don't mean just tonight.... I mean in just *finding* you."

That did it for Lisa. She felt like a stiff-necked fool...acting like that with a man with whom she had shared the closest encounter a man and woman could have. She smiled. "Thank you. I will. You're outrageous—" she walked toward him "—and impulsive—" she reached him and put her arms around his neck, kissing his left cheek, then his right as he beamed "—and absolutely marvelous."

"Starving, too," he kidded her. "And thirsty." He popped the cork from the bottle and poured champagne into two thin glasses. They went through the glass-clinking business and sipped. No toast seemed adequate, because both of them knew their eyes were saying it all. "Dinner, *dinner,* " he growled at her, and pulled two chairs up to the table.

"Be your guest," she quipped, serving them both from the covered dishes. "This present has almost destroyed my appetite. I'll scream if I can't try on a pair of earrings," she added, grinning.

He was taking her at her word, wolfing down chicken Kiev already, watching as she took the glittering stars from the case and debated which pair of studs to wear with them. Finally she opted for the brown diamonds and slipped the combination into her ears. "How's that?"

Nesbitt swallowed and said, "Gorgeous. Now eat your dinner before you waste away.... I want you just as you are."

She laughed and obeyed. The food was delicious, and she realized just how famished she'd been. They finished with sorbet. She remarked on its unusual flavor.

"Passion fruit," he explained, wriggling his brows and making a funny face.

She marveled at how easy they were together, how much at home she felt with him. It was incredible to remember that they'd only known each other for exactly one week. When she told him her thoughts, he said, "That's because this was...supposed to happen, Lisa." His expression was serious.

"Maybe it was," she answered, and reached across the table to touch him. He picked up her hand and kissed her palm with tenderness.

"I know it was. Remember what your book said about 'fatal opposites'?" He grinned at her. "And *vive les* opposites," he added, still clinging to her hand. After a moment he asked, "Do you feel like going out on the town...or would you rather laze around here tonight?"

"I don't feel like going out a bit. Lazing around sounds heavenly to me. How about you?"

He sighed with dramatic relief. "I'm so glad you said that, lady. I'm beat. It's perfect, just being here with you tonight."

"Then you don't want to trade me in for two twenties and a disco?" she teased him.

He swore mildly. "Heaven forbid." He laughed. Then he sobered a little, and added, "You know, that's one of the nicest things about this—that we're contemporaries. Not that there's any physical slowdown—" he grinned "—but it's a mental thing. We have the same...points of reference."

"I was thinking the very same thing," she told him companionably. "And speaking of points of reference, there's the greatest old movie on TV tonight."

"Let's watch it." She gathered up her gift and carried their coffee into the bedroom, which had its own TV set. While he telephoned room service to retrieve their dinner table, Lisa tidied up the bedroom and hung up his extra clothes.

She thought of how long it had been since she'd handled a man's clothes, and took a deep pleasure in it. Before she put the last garment on a hanger, she held it up to her cheek for a moment. Vaguely she noticed the sound of the table being wheeled out, and Nesbitt's amiable good night.

"Lisa. Oh, Lisa." She heard his voice from behind her and turned, smiling at him, feeling caught out in her sentimental gesture. But his eyes were tender. As he came toward her, holding out his arms, he said with a catch in his voice, "You're so...you're such a natural woman."

She basked in his strong embrace for the rest of the close, lazy evening, and throughout the long, intimate night.

Lisa woke early, feeling reborn. The first thing she saw was Mike's big arm, still around her relaxed body. It was very tanned in contrast to her lighter skin and the creamy color of her lace nightgown. She lowered her head and kissed his hand.

He stirred at once and snuggled closer to her, making a drowsy sound of happiness. She felt his warm mouth on the back of her neck, and he hugged her to him tightly. "Good morning," he mumbled. "A *very* good morning to you, Lisa." His breath was warm on her back. He nuzzled her between her shoulder blades.

"A very good morning," she murmured, and turned over to slide her arms around him. They kissed slowly and sweetly, and she knew that for both of them it was a moment of affection rather than desire. For some reason this affected her more deeply than physical longing itself.

She whispered that thought to him, and he smiled, looking inordinately pleased. "That's because everything with us is making love...like this—" he stroked her hair "—and this." He lightly kissed her nose and chin. "And this." He grasped her hand. She marveled that it was true; just holding his hand was more pleasurable than the act of love itself would have been with another man.

She said that aloud, and he held her close to him again, whispering, "I love you, Lisa. I know it already. You must have guessed that."

Lisa was overwhelmed with feeling, and she wanted desperately to say, "I love you, too." But even now, she didn't know. Not yet. The years of caution, her habit of self-analysis, got in her way. And she thought, of all things that I owe him, the first is utter honesty. I will never insult him by offering him less.

Instead of an answer she took his face between her hands and kissed every inch of it.

As if he knew what she was thinking, he said, "I'm glad you didn't say it back, lightly. I know it's too soon for you. It's all right, Lisa. It's all right, darling."

Their mouths met again for a long, long moment.

When she could speak, Lisa murmured, "You're a wonderful...wonderful man, Mike Nesbitt."

The sudden buzz of the extension by the bed startled them both. He waited discreetly for her to answer, handing her the receiver.

"Ma?" Of course, it was Charlie. "Did I call you too early? They get up with the horses around here."

Lisa tried to pull herself together. She was hearing her daughter's voice in a whole new way; she hadn't consciously thought of Charlie since yesterday morning. "No, I'm awake. How are you? Having fun?"

"Oh, *yes*. The horses are just great. We've been swimming and riding all the time. What did you do with yourself last night? Go honky-tonkin' with Dr. Heinz?" Charlie giggled.

Mike was getting up, as if he intended to tactfully leave her alone, but Lisa deterred him with her hand, smiling at him. They exchanged a tender look, and he lit a cigarette, leaning back in bed again. "I was with Mike, Charlie."

"Good. That must have been fun. When are you coming out here?"

"I don't mean it that way, Charlie. Mike and I have been together since last night." Lisa had never lied to her daughter, and she wasn't about to start now, she decided. She listened to the silence on the line uneasily. "Charlie?"

Now Lisa was aware of a restless motion from Mike and saw that he was getting up. With an affectionate touch on her arm, he blew a kiss at her and walked out of the room.

"Charlie?" Lisa repeated.

"I don't *believe* this, Mother." For one absurd moment Lisa felt as if their roles had been reversed; she heard shock and betrayal in the brash young voice. "You're always telling me not to...lose my cool. And now my own mother has lost hers."

Lisa was chagrined. "It's not like that, Charlie. And it's not something that can be discussed on the phone. We'll talk about it when I come to the ranch."

"And when will that be?" Charlie sounded cold, unreachable, and Lisa wished they were talking face-to-face. But this was the first time she'd been happy in more than a decade, and she'd be damned if she would apologize to anyone—including herself—for it.

"You don't understand, Charlie. You will when we talk about it," she said calmly.

"So when are you coming out here?" Charlie asked stubbornly, as if Lisa hadn't spoken.

"I'm not sure. There are a lot of things going on at the center."

"On the Fourth of July weekend?" Lisa could hear the skepticism in that.

"Yes. The space center's not a university, Charlie. I may be coming tomorrow. I'll let you know later today or tonight." Lisa added silently, I've been waiting for this weekend a lot longer than a week, and I'm going to have it.

"Okay, Mother."

"Charlie, are you all right, honey?"

"Sure," Charlie replied fliply. "You've left your excess baggage in good hands. I'll see you when I see you." She hung up.

Lisa stared at the receiver, then hung up, too.

"Trouble?" Mike was at the door, already dressed. She'd been subliminally aware of a shower running during her conversation with Charlie. Lisa smiled at him. He had an anxious, almost jealous expression.

"Nothing I can't handle. Children aren't always a total blessing," she said dryly. "I guess I should have waited to tell her. But we've always been honest with each other, and I couldn't bear to lie about this, Mike. Somehow it would...cheapen what happened to do that."

He sat down on the bed and took her in his arms, kissing the top of her head. "I'm so glad you feel that way, Lisa. Did she...ask when you were coming out to the ranch?"

Lisa nodded and told him what she'd replied.

"Thank you for that, too." His vivid eyes were shining; his reckless mouth was turned up at the corners with elation. "I want this weekend with you so much. I've got to be there Monday myself," he added. "I'm the official host at these Houstar affairs." He made a face and put his hand up to her cheek.

"You see, Colonel," she said, "my time has come. And I'm going to have it. There's a new amendment to my constitution...having to do with Mothers' Rights." He laughed with delight. "*And* I'm hungry. I know you are, too."

"You know me so well already. Shall we go out to eat?"

"I'd love to. But what about your work today?"

"That was make-work, beautiful," he admitted. "I don't have to go in at all. You know, I've been substituting work for living for too damned long." He hugged her.

"You're not the only one," she retorted. "I'm up to *here* with that. Let's play hooky, starting right now."

"You've got a deal. I'll order us some coffee while you get dressed."

She showered and got herself together quickly, taking an almost adolescent pleasure in deciding what to wear. She decided she'd match her clothes to her new jewels, rather than the reverse. Looking over the treasure trove again, she chose the Australian opals with their fiery blue-green, orange and gold lights, so she opted for a bright blue-green outfit that would be appropriate for just about anyplace.

After they'd had some coffee they went out to enjoy the new day. The air was marvelous, and they had a glorious time. They breakfasted at a quiet place in the museum district and then wandered through some of the museums. They had a light lunch, and Mike suggested that they go shopping in the luxurious mall. Lisa turned that down, saying she was feeling lazy. He picked up on that at once, and they went back to the hotel, where they made love again with a sweet hunger. It was such an exquisite evening that Lisa was fairly hypnotized with him. She felt that she'd never be able to do without him anymore, and was half-frightened, half-buoyed by that discovery. She reacted to him as if they'd known each other all their lives; there was almost a predestined ease between them.

They napped again, and when they woke decided to get into western gear and "docey-do" in one of the country-western spots. Mike teased her about hesitating to wear her diamond stars, saying that denim and diamonds were very big in Texas right now...and that besides, the "Lone Star" was never out of style. So in defiance of all her conservative habits, Lisa slipped the glittering stars, with ruby studs, into her ears. They looked delightfully daring with her red and brown western clothes.

She remembered that she'd promised to call Charlie and dialed the ranch, almost ashamed of her relief when Martha told her that Charlie had gone out with a crowd to dance. Lisa left the message that she'd be coming Monday.

When she went out with Mike, she felt absurdly carefree. They had a late, hilarious night and slept very late the next morning. "Feel like dressing up today?" he asked her on Sunday.

She said she did, so they both got into more formal clothes and went to a famous hotel where Sunday brunch was a Houston ritual. Lisa could hardly believe the elegance of the beautiful women or the elaborateness of the huge buffet—the whole scene was practically fictional. The tables, as the cliché went, groaned under the burden of great ice sculptures and too many kinds of foods to count.

They passed up the buffet table and went into the next room which featured made-to-order omelettes and the richest, darkest, best coffee Lisa had ever tasted. Replete, they wandered out to a movie and then to a cozy jazz club for a drink.

"And now?" Mike kissed her hand. They were sitting close together on a couch at a secluded table in dim, gentle light.

"I'm for a private dinner," she said softly. "I want to get away from it all...even when 'all' is as nice as this...on our last evening."

"*Last* evening?" His eyes expressed his shock. "I thought this was just the beginning." He squeezed her hand, staring at her.

"It is," she assured him. "I meant the last night of our weekend," she went on quickly, and saw his anxiety subside.

But it did seem like her last evening with him, somehow...before Monday morning, when she had to start being a mother again.

Chapter 6

But if Lisa had expected to step back into that role as soon as they reached the ranch, she was in for a surprise. It was already two o'clock, and she hadn't even talked to Charlie yet.

Martha had gone off to see about dinner, Mike was conferring with Frank about something, and Charlie was in the pool with a crowd of people. Lisa leaned back in her poolside chair and shut her eyes for a moment. She briefly reviewed the day since their arrival late that morning, a little exasperated with Charlie's maneuvers.

Lisa had been surprised not to see Charlie among the mass of people milling around under the awnings erected over the many picnic tables, or swimming in the pool. Frank and Martha had greeted her and Mike with affection; then Martha had told Lisa that Charlie must have lost track of the time, and was still out riding.

Then they'd immediately been swept into introductions and activity. Lisa had been dazzled, as she always was in Texas, by the bigness of it all—the enormous tables with the endless spread of various foods, the well-stocked bars, the huge dance floor set up for dancing to the infectious country music. A dozen people had claimed Mike's attention right away, and with an apology he had reluctantly left Lisa with Martha at one of the sheltered tables.

Lisa was glad she hadn't tried to "go western"; her cool lime-green sundress, with its narrow ivory stripes, felt good in the strong, shimmering heat. She had been looking forward to a confidential chat with Martha Harris, but that had turned out to be impossible. Martha, like Mike, was accosted by dozens of friends and acquaintances, some of whom, she told Lisa apologetically, she hadn't seen since the last Fourth of July. So naturally the talk had been general.

There were a lot of familiar faces in the crowd, Lisa found. At first she couldn't imagine why they were so familiar; then she recognized them as people from the center, looking quite different in their holiday gear. Chatting for a while with her sergeant-secretary, Lisa learned that the Fourth at the Houstar was quite a tradition. Mike still hadn't told her much about it; this morning, she recalled with pleased amusement, they'd had their minds on other things.

Finally she and Mike managed a brief time alone, when he asked her to dance.

It was delightful to be close to him, looking up into his bright blue eyes again, encircled in his arms. But she had to admit that the unshaded dancing area wasn't too comfortable. She'd almost forgotten, in the air-conditioned shelter of the hotel, the office and the places they'd been frequenting, how hot Texas could be.

"Confess." Mike smiled down at her. "This isn't your kind of thing."

"Not exactly," she admitted. "But it's... fascinating. I've never been to anything like this before. Or if I have, I was too young to remember. My family left Texas a long time ago."

He laughed at her polite evasion. "I must be getting soft myself. Right now I'd like to be alone with you in that nice cool jazz club...or better yet, the Seasons. Let's get some shade," he suggested.

They sat down at an unoccupied table, and he signaled to a passing waiter who was carrying a tray of ice-filled drinks. The man paused by their table; Mike took a julep and, after consulting Lisa, handed her a plain lemonade. She sipped it gratefully, feeling renewed.

"Damn," Mike said after sampling his julep, "I'm sorry I've had so little time for you today, honey. I knew it would be like this, which is why I put off coming earlier. I guess you're wondering how I got involved in all this—an astronaut on a ranch isn't exactly S.O.P. But then, we've been...discussing other things." He grinned at her.

"And how nice that is." She smiled back, excited all over again by the look in his eyes.

He took her hand. "Oh, yes. Yes," he agreed softly. "Well, you see," he went on in a more casual tone, "this place is a kind of sentimental...toy of my father's. And even if we've had our differences, it means something to me, too. My father's a tough old bird. He was born in the Panhandle—speaking of contrasts in Texas, you can fry an egg on the ground today, but in the winter on the Panhandle it gets so cold barbed wire snaps right in two. But back to my father. He was just a cowboy until he got himself a piece of land, and that land had oil under it. The rest is history. He went east, met my mother and settled in Florida. But later he built this place. My mother hated ranch life, so when things got...difficult between them he'd come back here to stay, and I visited sometimes when I was a kid. Then, when I got stationed in Texas, and later joined the space program, it seemed natural for me to act as host here. My dad's not well anymore, so he doesn't come back much." Mike paused, then added slowly, "I figured it was the least I could do, since I've never been the corporate type...and my association with Nesbitt's has been pretty random."

He smiled at her. "Except, of course," he concluded, "for sharing in the benefits. I rebelled against that, too, for a while, but my father's so old now I've mellowed. Besides, as you said, I'm not a saint, either. It's good to have money...especially when there's someone to spend it on." He squeezed her hand again and then seemed eager to dismiss the subject.

"But look, have you talked to Charlie yet?" he asked. "Where is she, anyway?"

"Martha said she was out riding; apparently she's practically lived on a horse since she's been here," Lisa said. "She's like that in New York—she rides a lot in Central Park. I hope she shows up soon."

Once more an acquaintance of Mike's appeared, and they were interrupted. Joining only vaguely in their conversation, Lisa mulled over what Mike had told her, thinking what an amazing life he'd had. For anyone to consider this enormous enterprise a "sentimental toy" was pretty overwhelming. It was so alien to her experience that she could hardly comprehend it.

Then Mike had to excuse himself again, saying something about a rodeo the following day.

"I'm glad you'll be back at work," she remarked, smiling. "Those things look so dangerous."

"I couldn't ride in one if I wanted to," Mike assured her. "They'd raise hell at the center if I broke a bone. I'd be in swell shape for a mission."

She had to laugh at the half-wistful way he sounded. But she herself was vastly relieved.

A little later Charlie suddenly appeared in a brief bikini, surrounded by Tony and three other people her age. She rushed over to Lisa to hug and kiss her, then rushed away again with a "See you later" and jumped into the pool.

When Lisa went inside to freshen up, she decided to steal a little private time and almost guiltily took off her shoes and stretched out on a chaise in one of the guest rooms. Enervated by the noise and heat, she fell asleep. She woke with a start, realizing it was nearly three o'clock. This was a great way, she thought, for a guest to behave. She got up and smoothed her hair, deciding to get into her swimsuit and cool off in the pool.

Mike had found her there a little while later. The crowd was thinning out; the few people left were all close friends of the Harris family. Charlie was gone again. Someone told Lisa that her daughter had gone to shower and change for dinner.

Lisa turned to Mike, who was stretched out in the pool chair next to hers, and said, "I think I'll have a word with Charlie."

He nodded. When Lisa got up and walked toward the pool house, she was aware of his gaze on her body in her tight maillot suit. After a quick shower she emerged again in her sundress, waving to Mike before heading for the house.

His eyes were full of tender affection, but she thought they looked anxious, too. He was worried about Charlie's reaction to *him*, Lisa thought.

That was such an unaccustomed idea that Lisa analyzed it all the way upstairs to the room where her daughter was staying. What would the future be like? She wondered if he was going to be jealous of Charlie. But he hadn't actually made a commitment, and if he didn't, Lisa was afraid she couldn't cope with *that,* either.

By the time she got to Charlie's room her head was pounding. She had to dismiss the other matters for now; the important thing was to reach her daughter again.

Lisa tapped at the door, heard Charlie call out, "Come in," and entered a spacious, airy room that looked very feminine and French with its touches of pink and lavender.

Charlie was sitting at the dressing table in her robe, arrested in the act of blow-drying her hair. When she saw Lisa she said coolly, "Hello, Ma," and went on with what she had been doing.

"Hello, stranger," Lisa said lightly. She shut the door and sat down in a big soft chair near the dresser. "How's it going? I haven't seen much of you today."

"I figured you'd be busy." Charlie put the dryer down and examined her hair critically in the mirror, still avoiding Lisa's eyes. She picked up her lip gloss and began applying it with close attention.

"Charlie, we've got to talk." Lisa fought her exasperation, keeping her voice low and calm. She waited patiently until her daughter was through with her lips. "Charlie?"

"What's to talk about, Ma? You checked me here," Charlie went on resentfully, "to get rid of me. And I'm here, out of your hair."

"Charlie, that's not true, and you know it." Lisa got up and stood behind Charlie, with her hands on her daughter's shoulders. "You were dying to stay; you told me so." Charlie made a restless movement, and Lisa dropped her hands.

Her daughter picked up her mascara and looked up at Lisa; the big blue-gray eyes were so much like Jack's, reflecting his old resentment. "Why didn't you tell me you had a thing for Mike?" Charlie demanded. "You didn't have to maneuver me this way."

Lisa sat down in the chair again and said, "It wasn't like that. Believe me, I was as surprised as you that this happened." She smiled, but Charlie wasn't looking at her; she was lightly applying mascara to her long, thick lashes.

"I'm mystified, kiddo," she added. "You must remember what you told me in New York—that I should get rid of Greg, whom you so delicately called a 'creep,' that I needed an Aries to jazz my life up." Lisa was still trying to keep it light, to cajole Charlie back into good humor.

"Well, I made a big mistake. At least when you were interested in Greg you still had time for me. But I have a feeling that those days are gone forever." Charlie got up and went to the chest of drawers, rummaging for a half slip, dropping the robe and stepping into the slip.

"Charlie, I'll always have time for you," Lisa protested.

Charlie was at the closet now, looking through dresses. Her back was turned and her voice muffled when she retorted, "You didn't have much time for me this weekend." Finally she chose a pale blue sundress and began to put it on. She struggled with the back zipper.

"Let me help you with that." Lisa went to her and started to zip up the dress, but Charlie shrugged away from her.

"I can do it." She zipped herself up. Her expression of stiff resentment had not relaxed. "As a matter of fact, I'd better get used to doing things for myself."

"You always have," Lisa said reasonably. "What's different now?"

Charlie just looked at her.

"Look, why don't you come back with us this evening?" Lisa suggested.

"Are you kidding? And spoil your little fling?"

"It's not a fling, Charlie."

Her daughter was on her knees by the bed, muttering, "Where are those lousy sandals?" She held up the bedspread to look. Finally she retrieved the sandals and slipped them on her bare feet.

She stood up again and faced Lisa. "So when are you guys going to get married?"

If there was one thing Lisa detested, it was the youthful habit of referring to men and women indiscriminately as "guys," and Charlie knew it. Lisa was aware that her daughter was trying to irritate her.

Repressing the comment that a marriage of two "guys" sounded like a very odd arrangement, Lisa answered calmly, "You know very well that I wouldn't jump into anything like that this soon."

"Well, it sure didn't take you long to jump into bed."

Lisa almost slapped her; it took all her control not to. "That's enough, Charlie. Don't you think all this is a little silly? You're being totally inconsistent. You'll be going to the Cape sometime this summer, then you'll be going away to school. And you didn't get upset over that. You're a grown woman now, and you're acting like a spoiled little girl."

"This is different. You're different, and you don't even realize it. You've changed already," Charlie accused her.

"Not about you. I'll never change how I feel about you," Lisa said gently, taking Charlie in her arms. But the young body was stiff, resistive. "Come on, Charlie. Why don't you go back to Houston with us tonight?"

"Not on your life. I'm going to stay here, where I'm really wanted. And then at the end of the week I'm going to the Cape. I've already called Dad about it. At least *he'll* have time for me—he always does." Charlie was back at the dresser again, checking out her appearance, straightening the scattered items of makeup.

Lisa winced, thinking how unfair that was, how hurtful a child could be. Jack would be oh so sympathetic about Lisa's "neglect" and probably hint ever-so-gently that she'd always put her career ahead of her daughter. She wondered where all their closeness had gone so suddenly, all that marvelous closeness they'd enjoyed in New York, when they were more like friends than parent and child.

"Look, Ma, I've got to go. I promised Tony and George I'd dance some more before dinner."

Lisa nodded, feeling defeated. The "great advisor" could certainly use some advice right now herself. It was a pretty ironic situation. "Okay. So you won't come with us tonight?"

"No, thanks. I don't want to be the one to make a crowd." Charlie walked out and shut the door gently.

Lisa wandered around the room for a moment, then sat at the dresser, feeling like crying. What a mess all this was—to have the chance of happiness for the first time in so long, but to take that chance at the expense of what she valued so highly: the love of her own child. It wasn't fair, and Lisa felt she'd handled it all so badly.

She sighed, and thought, so be it. She wouldn't push Charlie any more right now. Maybe later in the week she'd feel different. Lisa got up and went out, going slowly downstairs to join the others on the terrace.

Mike knew something was wrong as soon as he saw her. "What's up?" he asked her softly, taking her aside. He'd changed into a shirt and jeans again, and he looked bigger and more imposing than ever, and very protective. Lisa wanted to go right into his arms then and there to be hugged and comforted.

But she only said, "I'm afraid Charlie's not taking it all too well."

"I'm sorry, honey. Do you think maybe I...should say something to her?"

"That would be the worst possible thing right now." Noticing his hurt expression, she decided that that was the worst possible thing *she* could have said, too. "I didn't mean it that way," she assured him hastily. "I meant, we should just let her stew a while," she added with a shaky smile.

"Whatever you say." He still didn't look reassured, though, Lisa saw, and she was assailed with new anxiety. She had an unhappy feeling that this was just the beginning of their problems.

Dinner was not an easy affair. Charlie was bright and talkative, Mike was tense and Lisa uncomfortable, sensing a veiled hostility between the two people she cared most about. The others seemed to have picked up on it, too. When they were leaving, Lisa tried to cover things up by saying to Charlie casually,

"Have fun. I know you'll enjoy the rodeo," as if that were the main reason Charlie was staying on. Charlie allowed Lisa to kiss her on the cheek, but when Lisa added, "I'll be in touch," Charlie lifted her brows in an exasperating fashion and, when Mike moved toward her as if ready to give her cheek a kiss, too, deftly evaded him.

Lisa and Mike were both very quiet on the drive back to the city, making random, almost impersonal comments about the day.

Then, when the skyline of Houston was coming into view, Lisa gasped.

"What is it?" Mike glanced swiftly at her, then back at the highway. "What's the matter, honey? Is it still Charlie?"

"Not Charlie, Mike. Something's the matter with my *brain.*" She'd completely forgotten to tell him about her father's letter. Friday night, of course, it had slipped her mind altogether, and then after the disturbing conversation with Charlie on Saturday, she'd been preoccupied with that. She'd been carrying the letter with her, transferring it from bag to bag, half meaning to bring it up and then, when she had the opportunity, forgetting again.

She told him, briefly and succinctly, detailing the gist of the letter.

Mike was very excited, everything else crowded from his mind by the information. "Good Lord, Lisa...a Marley inspiration. Why didn't I think of that? But then, you said he's been ill, living in seclusion, and..."

He paused. She could hear the questions in his tone. As they neared the hotel she told him the whole story, slowly, carefully—about her father's searing guilt after the astronauts' tragic death; the gradual erosion of his genius; the breakdown and confinement; the wonderful news of his recovery and imminent release.

Mike braked in front of the Golden Seasons. He surrendered the car to the attendant absently and rushed her through the lobby to the elevator. As soon as they were in the suite, he said, "Now, let me see that letter, please."

She took it from her bag and handed it to him.

He read it intently, still standing, first skimming it with enormous eagerness, then sitting down to read it with greater care twice more before he said a word.

When he looked up at her his eyes were fiery again, blazing with energy and new enthusiasm.

"Darling, this is fantastic. I can't wait to check this out tomorrow. In fact, I think I'll call some of the guys right now; maybe I can catch them at home."

He took an address book from his hip pocket and consulted it. He began to make his calls.

Lisa went into the bedroom to change, thinking, at least something seems to be going right.

But she wasn't so sure the next morning when she and Mike walked into the admin building together and were confronted at once by the detestable Rayburn.

"Well, good *morning*," Rayburn said with a nasty inflection. "I heard you people have been burning the midnight fuel."

Lisa was annoyed by the rush of heat to her face. Could he possibly have heard something? Then she remembered Mike's calls.

"I appreciate your phoning my men instead of me, Nesbitt." Rayburn shot a resentful glance at Mike.

"There was no answer at your house; you were out, if you recall, Jim." Mike's tone was even, which only served to irritate Rayburn more.

"Well, you could have waited, pal. I *am* the head of the engineering end of the project." Rayburn glared at Mike, then gave Lisa an insulting up-and-down look.

Mike caught the look and bristled. "We've already been waiting for quite a while to clear this thing up, Rayburn. And besides, I can't count on your cooperation. You've laughed off the possibility of engineering problems from Day One. You'd love it if the fault's in me and my men, wouldn't you...so your team can get the flight?"

"Mike..." Lisa murmured and touched his arm. She realized it was the first time she'd used his given name in front of Rayburn.

Rayburn smiled unpleasantly and raised his brows. "If you're accusing me of a cover-up, Nesbitt, it occurs to me that you might have been covering up an interesting item yourself." He gave Lisa another one of his undressing glances, and she noticed with apprehension that Mike was getting madder and madder.

"I'm going to give you a break, Rayburn; I'm not going to try to understand what you mean." Mike's voice had a steely resonance and his hands were clenched.

"If you'll excuse me," Lisa murmured, trying to create a diversion, "I'd better get to my office."

Mike put his hand on her elbow. "I'll walk with you; I'd like to have a word with Heinz." Ignoring Rayburn, he steered Lisa around the corner and down the hall toward her cubicle.

"That son of a...seacook is going to go too far pretty soon, and I'll have to do something about it," he muttered to Lisa.

"Please, Mike. Try to let it go for a while. I have a feeling we're going to have enough trouble without a...set-to between the top brass." She kept her tone purposely light, hoping to kid him out of his rage. "What do you want to talk to Dieter about, by the way?" Looking up at him, Lisa decided that her diversion hadn't done much good; he was still furious.

"Nothing, right now. I just had to get away while the going was good," Mike admitted. "I didn't want to deck that...deck Rayburn while you were around. I've got the shortest fuse in the program," he added, smiling down at her. "I'm going to the lab right now and check out your father's theory with the guys. I wanted to cool down before I see Rayburn again."

She was glad to see that his face had relaxed a little. Smiling up at him she said, "Well, take it slow, Colonel. Hold it together. We'll smooth it out soon."

He laughed at her use of astronaut slang and bent down to kiss her lightly on the nose in the empty corridor. "See you at lunch if I can make it, honey."

"Wonderful." Watching him walk away, she began to feel better; whatever else happened, they still had that magical, private wonder that was all their own. With any luck, it could go on and on...except for Charlie.

The thought of the conflict with her daughter reawakened Lisa's anxious gloom. Now, besides the problem with the project and Charlie, there was also the new trouble with Rayburn. It was obvious that he knew about her and Mike, and that was going to be very awkward. Rayburn could use it against them, claiming that Lisa's emotional involvement with Mike Nesbitt negated her objectivity.

Her feelings were in a turmoil when she opened her door and walked through the sergeant's cubicle. She managed to compose her expression, though, and ask how her secretary's weekend had gone.

Lisa shut her own door and sat down at her desk, plunging into her schedule for the week's tests. She decided that the first thing to do would be to confer with Heinz; the new engineering tests based on her father's theory must be made known to her colleague right away. Knowing how much he'd looked forward to his long weekend rest, she hadn't wanted to bother him at home. Now she buzzed his office.

"Dieter? How was your holiday?"

"Excellent, my dear." Heinz sounded alert and rested. "I closed myself off in air-conditioned splendor with books and Bach and Schumann, far, far away from those vulgar boom-crackers of your countrymen."

She laughed at his word for firecrackers. "Well, it's back to the grind now. May I come to your office? I have some good news for you."

He said that he would come to her, because she had some records he wanted to examine. In just a few moments he entered, smiling. His old eyes were twinkling with curiosity.

"So...what is this news, my dear Lisa?" He sat down, peering at her. "I must say, you don't look as if you've been on holiday. Is anything the matter?"

"Not...exactly," she faltered.

"Well. Later you will tell me, in your own good time, what that vague expression really means. But before I pry it out of you—" he chuckled "—you are going to talk of other matters."

"Yes." She told him about her father's letter and the new direction the engineering tests might be taking.

Heinz nodded, beaming. He was one of the few people in on the secret of her father's illness. "I knew that my friend Philip would be well again. This seems to prove it. I can't tell you, my child, how delighted I am. I know you share my delight."

"Oh, Dieter, I can't tell you how much." She smiled widely. But her smile died when she remembered the other matters confronting her.

"But...?" he prompted, smiling. "But we must continue our own tests for the time being...*and* there's something bothering you. Personally. What is it, Lisa?"

She hesitated. The trouble with Rayburn, Charlie's alienation, were things she ought to be able to work out herself. But she realized how silly it was not to confide in Dieter Heinz, who had always been so close to her father and to her. "I suppose," she began slowly, "it all begins with...Mike Nesbitt."

Heinz nodded wisely. "Oh, I know about that, my dear."

"You know?"

He smiled almost pityingly. "Oh, Lisa, it would be plain to a blind man that there has been a...tenderness between you two from the beginning. I felt—what is it the young Americans are so fond of saying?—the 'vibes' between you." Heinz made a comical, triumphant sound that was like a growling chortle. "Come now, did you think you could pull the woolly over old Dieter's eyes, when I have examined so many people?"

"The *wool,* Dieter," she corrected, giggling.

"Thank you." He had asked her to correct his Americanisms when he stumbled over them. "Well, did you?"

She shook her head.

"So, I assume that matters have...progressed," he added in his delicate way. She nodded. "But that's splendid," he protested. "You have been divorced—

what is it?—years now. And you and this young man seem admirably suited. So where is the problem?''

Lisa told him about Charlie, then about the suspected problem with Rayburn.

''Ah, yes, that neurotic major. He may well be a problem,'' Heinz conceded. ''But as to your daughter, I can see no problem there. She is a young woman now, not a little girl. She will be going to school, perhaps contracting an alliance of her own. Don't you think that perhaps your guilt about the failed marriage has caused you to...coddle her a bit too much, treat her like a child when she is not? Come now, admit it. You are a doctor and a brilliant woman, Lisa...you are also a mother. I know so well the fierce protectiveness of the maternal creature. How like tigers you are with your cubs,'' he twitted.

Lisa was annoyed. ''I think that's absurd,'' she protested. ''Charlie is a perfectly normal child.... She's independent, and healthy, and...''

''So, you see, you still call her a child. Now don't get on your tall horse, Lisa...''

This time she was too irritated to correct his English and let him go on.

''...But listen to me. Of course your daughter is lovely, healthy and quite sound. But I think she is a little too attached to you. It's time she learned the world does not revolve around her, that she is not your sun and moon...not she only. That she will find her *own* sun and moon as you have. That you have the right to your own life. Am I not right?''

Lisa thought about it. There was a lot of truth in what he said. Perhaps her guilt *had* made her defer to Charlie a bit more than other mothers did to their daughters. Charlie had been the reason she hadn't married Greg, or so she'd thought until now. In that case her daughter had done her the biggest favor of her life. Lisa grinned, feeling lighter now that she'd unburdened herself. Of all people, she thought, a psychiatrist should have realized the value of that act.

"Now that I have solved that part of your life," Heinz said in the self-mocking way she enjoyed so much, "the other matter, the thing with Rayburn, may be a little more complicated. You are absolutely right in assuming he will use this against you and Nesbitt if he can. The best way to scotch that, at the moment, is to continue our work as conscientiously as possible. Do you agree?"

"I do indeed," she answered with fervor. "And thank you, Dieter."

"It's all in a day's work. Now—let's get to it."

They dived into the schedule at once and proceeded with that day's testing. Lisa discovered that Heinz had been right: now that they were in the swing of it, the complicated new procedures went much more quickly.

Lisa and Heinz were so preoccupied that they worked right through lunch. She hadn't heard from Mike at all. Presumably he was just as busy. She couldn't wait to hear the results of his preliminary meeting with the engineers.

Lisa was having a sandwich at her desk at about three when her buzzer sounded. It was Mike.

"What's happened?" she asked him eagerly.

"Plenty." He sounded jubilant. "I'm sorry about lunch."

"It doesn't matter. Tell me about it," she urged him.

"I won't go into the whole thing now; I don't have time. The gist of it is, it looks good. There are still plenty of wrinkles, but it looks like your father's put his finger on it, Lisa."

She felt terrifically elated. "Oh, Mike, that's sensational."

"You're damned right, Rayburn's about to have an aneurysm." She heard his hearty laugh; it fairly rattled the receiver. "But look, first things first—How soon can you get away?"

She told him.

"I'll have to accept that. I'll pick you up at your office, then. And look, I want to call your father. May I? I'm being very...discreet about the whole thing, you understand...but I need his number."

"Of course." She gave it to him. "He'll be overjoyed. And Mike, give him my love, will you?"

"Well—" she could hear the smile in his voice "—what you can spare from *me.*"

She said goodbye softly and hung up, caught in a whole new kaleidoscope of feelings—delight over the direction the project was taking, the confirmation that her father's gifts had not been lost...and the last thing Mike had said. "What you can spare from *me*."

When he'd murmured that, she'd known with a deep, warm certainty that she *did* love him. That was a wonderful and dazzling piece of knowledge.

And yet the way he'd put it gave her pause, left her with a gnawing uncertainty in the midst of her happiness. Would his love be so possessive, so demanding, that he would be jealous of her whole family? She remembered his saying that he'd resolved never to have children, to find a wife who would belong just to him.

Perhaps it couldn't work. Maybe Mike Nesbitt couldn't cope with a woman whose loyalties to her daughter and her parents, especially to her father, were so close and strong.

She reproached herself. She was reading too much into a few words, and if there was anything they didn't need right now, it was an extra, *invited* worry. So she thrust the idea away and went determinedly back to work, eager to finish by the time she was supposed to meet Mike.

The time sped by; before she could believe it, they were driving back to Houston.

Mike was enthusiastically detailing his conversation with her father when she involuntarily gasped.

"What is it?" he asked, a bit impatiently, she thought, because he was right in the middle of a critical bit in his report.

"I forgot to call Charlie." Except for the talk with Heinz, she'd hardly given Charlie a thought all day.

"Can't that wait?" Mike demanded. This time he didn't bother to hide his impatience. "Surely you want to hear about this."

"Of course," she said. "I'm sorry. Please...go on, Mike." But she wasn't all that sorry; she was a little impatient now herself. Didn't he realize that she had other concerns besides the project?

She listened absently as he finished. By the time they got to the hotel, some of her earlier pleasure had lessened and she felt curiously restless.

She told Mike to go ahead and shower; it would be a good time to call Charlie. When Lisa spoke to her, Charlie was only mildly enthusiastic about the news of her grandfather's part in the project. She was still cold and sulky, saying that she planned to go straight to the Cape on Friday.

"Straight to the Cape?" Lisa demanded with exasperation. "What about..." She had started to say, "What about seeing me before you go?" but she changed it to "What about all your things, Charlie?" Something in her prevented her from groveling any more, especially to her own daughter.

When Charlie responded, "You're so sentimental, Mother," in a sarcastic way, Lisa wondered if she'd been too cool. "Of course I'm going to come for my things, for Pete's sake. Tony or George will drive me. I'll come during the day when you're out so I won't be in your hair. You don't have to pack for me."

That did it for Lisa. She couldn't allow this alienation to continue. "Charlie," she said in a softer tone, "let's not talk to each other like this. It's never been this way with us, honey; I can't understand it. This isn't you. And it's *certainly* not me. Look, Charlie, we've got to talk some more, face-to-face. Why don't you come back here...please?"

"And interfere with your life?" Charlie countered. "That'll be the day."

Lisa hesitated just a fraction too long. When it came down to it, it *would* interfere with her life, but she couldn't say so.

"You see?" Charlie sounded coldly, painfully vindicated. "You can't answer that, Mother. No, thanks."

"Then let me come there," Lisa suggested as calmly as she could manage. "We've got to talk this out."

"We can talk till doomsday and it'll be the same thing, all over again. You've got your work and your...friend Mike Nesbitt, and I'm just excess baggage."

"You keep saying that, Charlie, and it still comes up wrong," Lisa argued. "This is just a few weeks in our lives. I'll be alone nine months of the year, when you're at school. Or you could meet someone in college, fall in love and get married. Where would that leave me?"

"Where you were before," Charlie retorted. "Pretty happy, it seemed to me. Independent. Now you're letting some man foul up our lives. That's all I know."

"You're not thinking straight, Charlie," Lisa responded calmly. "And you know it. But right now the important thing is for us to talk before you go running off to the Cape."

"I'm sorry, Mother. There won't be time. I've already told Dad when I'd arrive. And there are things I've said I'd do here at the ranch for the rest of the week."

Lisa sighed, exhausted with the whole thing all of a sudden. "We'll talk again," she promised.

"Oh, sure," Charlie said fliply and hung up.

Lisa stood with the receiver still to her ear, numbly listening to the dead line.

Then she felt Mike's arms around her, his body pressed to hers. He was nuzzling the back of her neck. For the first time in their acquaintance her body did not immediately respond. She felt like crying; there was a hard aching knot in her throat.

She replaced the receiver as his arms tightened around her waist. "All done?" he murmured against her hair.

"*Done* is the word. Oh, Mike." She turned and leaned against him, realizing that he was wearing only a towel tied about his muscular waist. His chest was broad and consoling. She leaned her face against it, inhaling the clean pine-soap scent of his hair-roughened, tanned skin, enjoying the sensation of being sheltered, comforted.

"Umm..." His hands were stroking her sides. "You smell delicious, like a bed of roses. Speaking of beds..."

She looked up into his eyes. They were very bright, and his mouth was smiling, expectant. "Lovely Lisa," he said softly.

Suddenly he seemed incredibly insensitive, so involved in his own desires that it chilled her. He hadn't even asked her about the result of her conversation. But then, taking her by surprise, he asked, "What's wrong? More trouble from Houstar?"

She nodded, reproaching herself for what she'd been thinking. "I can't get through to Charlie, Mike."

"I'm sorry to hear that, honey." She relaxed against him again. Now his body, rather than his mouth and eyes, expressed his true concern; his hands were caressing her again, and it was very clear that Mike Nesbitt had only one thing on his mind.

"Mike..." she said gently. "I need to...relax a little, take a shower, and..."

"Now?" he protested, his lips grazing her brow and cheekbone.

"Yes."

"All right, darling. I guess you have had quite a day. I'll wait for you...in my favorite room." He grinned and gave her an intimate pat. "Go shower."

Still feeling uneasy and nervous, she walked with him into the bedroom. He threw himself on the bed, smiling at her as she got a robe from the closet. It seemed somehow symbolic that she didn't undress before him, but put the robe over her arm and went to the bathroom still clothed. The shower didn't do much to relax her. With an awful sensation of detachment she dried and scented her body, put on the robe and went back to the bedroom.

"My, my, we're so formal, Doctor." Usually when he called her that she responded by calling him Colonel, but this time she didn't feel like it. She noticed that his towel was draped over a chair; he was lying under the sheet up to his narrow waist. The sight of his strong, tanned torso melted her for an instant, but when his smile died and he got that impatient look again, she felt herself cool.

Maybe, she thought, I've made a horrible mistake. Maybe what I've been feeling is just an overwhelming physical attraction. Maybe she shouldn't have told Charlie about it so soon. It was possible that she'd alienated her own child because of a fleeting encounter.

"Lisa..." He looked disturbed, uneasy now. "Come here. Something's really bothering you, and you've got to tell me what it is." He held out his arms to her.

When he did Lisa felt that melting warmth again. She went to the bed and sat down next to him, but she didn't take off her robe.

"Oh, darling, not like that," he protested. "Lie down by me. Let me hold you."

She obeyed, grateful for the strength of his arms, but not yet relaxing.

"You feel so tight," he whispered. "Want me to rub your neck?" He started to do that. Confused, she realized that she had become even stiffer.

"No, Mike. No...thank you." His hand dropped away from her neck, and he sighed.

"Okay." He took his arms away and leaned over to get a cigarette from the table. "Talk to me," he commanded, lighting the cigarette, exhaling and leaning back on the pillows.

Her body was loosening a bit now, and she leaned back, too, on the neighboring pillows. "We've got problems, Mike."

"We've also got a lot of good things going for us, Lisa," he reminded her with a hint of his earlier impatience. "First of all, we've got this..." He reached over and took her hand. "And we've got a light at the end of the tunnel about the project."

"And we've got Rayburn, and Charlie, and..." she countered.

"Rayburn and Charlie, I agree. It's the 'and' that bothers me." He squeezed her hand. She turned and looked at him.

"Mike, I'm very...confused."

He frowned. "What about? Not *us,* Lisa. Not that."

Just as she had with Charlie, Lisa hesitated an instant too long. He picked up on it immediately. She saw his lips tighten, the joy going out of his eyes like a slowly diminishing light. "I see."

"No, Mike, you don't. I just need a little time alone. To think about things." As soon as she'd said that, Lisa wished she could recall the words.

Chapter 7

From the expression on his face, the controlled tightness of his lips and the shut quality of his glance, she knew she'd hurt him. Disproportionately, it was true, but all the same he was deeply pained.

"I do see. What you're saying is that you'd like me to leave."

"No, I..." She did need to be alone, just for a little while. His physical magnetism, his very presence, filled all the spaces, made it impossible for her to think.

"Oh, yes, you..." he mocked her with a one-sided grin. "It's a kid's way to handle things, Lisa," he added sharply. "Adults stay and talk things out."

Now she was mad. How dare he lecture her on what was adult, with his juvenile attitude toward love and commitment...with his ideas on parenthood and responsibility?

"I hardly think," she began coolly, "that you're an expert on adulthood."

He winced; a spark of anger lit his vivid blue eyes. "Now I really do see," he responded in a hard voice. "I'm not 'adult' because I haven't let some kid eat me alive and run my life for me, the way you have, Lisa."

"Mike, please don't say any more," she pleaded.

"I won't, lady. If you want loneliness and silence, you've got it." She remembered too late how short his fuse was; he had warned her about it himself. She wanted to say something, even to apologize, but the words died in her throat.

He was on his feet now, dressing swiftly, not looking at her. And then he was walking out of the room. She heard the front door of the suite slam.

The silence and solitude she had wanted had turned to a deathlike stillness now, a yawning loneliness. The tears were coming, and she let them come.

Mike Nesbitt swore and strode down the garden-lined corridor; the bright blossoms were only a blur. He jabbed at the elevator button savagely, noticing that the damned thing had passed this floor and was going down. He paced while he waited for a car to stop.

Then he stopped in mid stride and headed back toward Lisa's suite. He stopped again. No, damn it, he was not going to crawl to her. Walking out of that bedroom had been like walking away from everything in life that mattered. But he couldn't stay when she so plainly didn't want him there. It was unlikely that she'd want him any more if he went back right now.

Mike walked back to the elevator bank; there was an actual ache in his chest, as if he'd taken a hard punch to the body, and he was having hell's own time just swallowing. It would be swell, he decided wryly, for a man of his age and rank to lose his dignity in a hotel elevator. His mouth jerked, and he put up his hand to stop it.

By the time the elevator came he was okay again. But all the way through the lobby and into his car, he could think of only one thing: he should have stood his ground and hung on to that short fuse of his.

I wonder what's going to happen now, Lisa asked herself dully when the paroxysm of weeping was over. At least she felt relieved. If anyone should know the therapeutic value of tears, she judged, it was someone in her line of work.

She began to move around automatically, straightening up the bedroom. The sight of Mike's discarded towel gave her a momentary pang, but she picked it up and took it to the bathroom to hang it up.

Probably part of her deep depression was simply a blood-sugar thing; she'd had almost no lunch, and now it was long past dinnertime. Without anticipation she ordered dinner. When it arrived she found it as unappetizing as she had expected. Nevertheless she made herself eat a sensible amount and found it helped a little.

After dinner was cleared away, she restlessly roamed the suite, thinking how very empty it was without Charlie...without Mike. She threw herself down on the couch and leaned her head back, reliving the first night in Houston, the night when she and Mike had first made love.

She remembered with a queer little catch in her heart how he had called her "Golden Lisa"...how golden the light had been on his hard, splendid body; his lean hips, his deeply tanned and powerful legs; how the hair on his body had looked like red gold. How vulnerable his mouth had been, how fiery his blue eyes. And most of all she remembered the wild, sweet pleasure his skilled and tender caresses had aroused in her body; the speechless wonder of their ultimate fulfillment.

She ached for him.

Yet all that was a purely physical magic, and she had been alone and starved too long. What about the rest of it?

The rest of it, she had to concede after sober reflection, was almost perfect. Almost.

There was still his dismaying possessiveness, the demand that she make him, and only him, the center of her life. On the other hand, what else were a man and woman supposed to be to each other? Maybe Mike was completely right and she herself completely wrong.

It was true that she'd never had that experience. Her marriage to Jack had certainly been far from ideal. Even her first wild infatuation with him had never been anything like the undying love she'd wistfully read and wondered about. There must be an answer somewhere, but she didn't have it now.

She decided to find something to read, something to help her stop thinking for a while, and got up to examine the books she'd brought with her. Among them, of course, was *The House of Stars*.

Oh, no, not *that*. It would only remind her more of the him and their dilemma. She had picked it up, and now she started to replace it. But somehow she couldn't resist. She took it with her to the bedroom, turned on the bedside lamp and began to read the first section once more, the love story of the Libra woman and the Aries man.

It was almost eerie now to read the passage which described the fictional hero's gift to his beloved—the ancient, hornlike symbol of Aries in diamonds, the birthstone of those born in April. Mike had given *her* diamonds, the delicate diamond stars, with all the wonderful studs for centers, like the hearts of glittering dream flowers.

Lisa considered all over again how impulsive he'd been to choose such an extravagant gift for a woman he'd met only the day before...but also how imaginative, how considerate. What care he must have taken, she reflected; she could picture him consulting for a long time with a jeweler, and above all showing an almost psychic understanding of her tastes by his choices. That incredible gift had been a symbol of his imagination, his uniqueness. How many men could have thought of such a thing, she wondered.

The answer was not one in a thousand.

And not one man in a thousand could have attracted, touched, aroused and fulfilled her as Mike Nesbitt had. It seemed insane to throw such a rare gift away, to pass up what might be her one chance for the greatest happiness she'd ever known.

Why should I, she agonized. She picked up the book again. She found her eyes flying over the rest of the story of love, discovering new likenesses between it and her own situation.

Maybe that was the problem, she decided. Maybe what they had shared was just as unreal as what she'd been reading about. She had thought in New York that she was still entitled to be carried away. Well, now she had been, and it wasn't perfect. The heroines of love stories didn't have her responsibilities to cope with.

It was a dismaying conclusion.

She was startled by the buzz of the phone by her bed. Her heart hammered; it had to be Mike. Her hands were shaking a little when she picked up the receiver.

"Lisa?" It was the crisp, matter-of-fact tone of Greg Hamilton. Her heart fell.

"Greg," she answered coolly, knowing her voice must reflect her disappointment.

"I assume I didn't call too late," he said, "since it's earlier there." He was always so damned correct, she thought, amused at her own perversity. Not two minutes before she had been thinking Mike was "unreal." Heaven knew, Greg was anything but, and now that irritated her. "How are things going?"

"Very well," she lied. "And with you?"

She hardly listened to his answer, and when he asked her more questions about the project, she found herself telling him about it with even greater enthusiasm, praising everything about her colleagues, the center and Texas.

"I see," he said in a noncommittal, flat way. "So, are you going to go on one of those flights, Lisa? I assumed that was really why you ran off with nothing more than a postcard." She'd sent him a card the first morning in Houston.

She repeated silently, a flight. She'd totally forgotten about that in her preoccupation with other things, and that in itself was astonishing.

"Not yet," she said calmly. "After all, I've hardly been here any time at all."

"So when do you think you'll be coming back?"

She felt a rush of frustration. Greg hadn't said a word about missing her, caring for her. It occurred to her again how much like Jack he was: proper and controlled and civilized. Too damned civilized.

Lisa felt like saying, "Don't be *too* overwhelmed with emotion." Now more than ever she saw her association with Greg for what it had always been: he was a straw she'd grasped at to keep from drowning in loneliness. And what a dry, stiff straw at that. He was as unlike Mike Nesbitt as a gas range was to a volcano.

She answered, "I really don't know at this point. I could be here another month, or longer."

There was a brief pause; then Greg said in his flat way, "I see. You sound...different, Lisa. Is everything all right?"

"Everything is fine," she assured him falsely.

"I'm glad," he said a bit more warmly. "Well, let me know how things go...and when you're coming back."

"I'll do that, Greg. It was nice of you to call."

When they'd hung up, she reviewed their conversation. Her first thought was one of amazement—amazement that she'd ever bothered with the man at all. Then she remembered his asking if she were all right.

She *wasn't* all right. Aside from all her other problems, she hadn't even thought of a flight since she came to Houston. And why? Because she'd been so mesmerized by Mike Nesbitt that when they were together he drove every other consideration right out of her mind. Painfully she felt her old skepticism, her early suspicions. Had the mention of a flight been a ploy on Mike's part to get her to Houston...just as his phony interest in her daughter had been a ploy to get her alone, and into bed?

She couldn't believe that, not now. There were too many other, wonderful things to outweigh her doubts.

And there were several things she was perfectly sure of: one was that she'd never see Greg Hamilton again, no matter what happened with Mike Nesbitt. The other was that it was absurd to value "reality" that highly: good heavens, space flight itself seemed dreamlike, and any woman who wanted to go into space couldn't care that much for being sensible.

Lisa smiled for the first time in hours as she considered her own conclusion.

There was something else, too. She already missed Mike more than she'd ever missed anyone in her whole life. When tomorrow came, if she had to be the peacemaker, she would. She could no longer imagine her life without him.

Right now, though, she felt drained, exhausted. She was going to take the phone off the hook and go to sleep.

When she reached her office a little later than usual the next morning, she found a note on her desk indicating that he had telephoned. Lisa's spirits rose. It was only a matter of time now, she thought exultantly, before it was all straightened out again. It might be a tough row to hoe, with all that confronted them. Nevertheless they would work it out; they *had* to.

Having been summoned to another high-level conference, Lisa went into the meeting room feeling renewed and in command. She saw the center's deputy director taking his place to preside; Heinz was on hand, with Rayburn and the higher echelon of engineers.

And Mike.

Lisa smiled at him with open warmth after she had acknowledged the others, and saw the mingled chagrin and joy in his eyes. She was so glad to see him, so eager for the conference to be over, that she had to discipline herself sternly to follow what was going on.

That in itself was so amazing, so unlike her usual professional detachment, that she knew how silly their brief separation had been.

But when she heard Rayburn speaking, her attention snapped back to the matter at hand. "I understand that Dr. Heron has expressed a wish to enter the simulated capsule herself. This is extremely unprecedented and, I think, interruptive to the project."

Lisa saw Mike frown and opened her mouth to speak. Before she could, Richard Gould, the engineering chief, beat her to it. She liked Gould, who was a great admirer of her father's as well as a brilliant and eminently fair man. Secure in his position, Gould never minced or wasted words. "Nonsense, Jim," he said easily. "Lisa's an MIT woman as well as a psychiatrist, so the idea is sound on two scores. I think it's a great idea, and we're setting it up for tomorrow."

"I wouldn't do that without a lot of extra checking," Rayburn insisted, as if she weren't even present. "She hasn't been subjected to this kind of thing before. Women usually aren't."

Mike spoke up sarcastically. "Your anxiety is touching, Jim. I can't believe I'm hearing this. I'd like to remind the major of those tests using twenty-seven civilian women, several of whom were in their sixties. The women were superior to the men, if you recall, in adapting to the physical and psychological hardships. Women need less oxygen, and they're more radiation-resistant than we are. That was fifteen *days;* what we're talking here is about three hours."

"Dr. Heron has not been in recent training," Rayburn said huffily.

"Come now, Jim," the deputy director intervened. "I have Dr. Heron's records here. She had her physical-psychological last week; she's in top shape."

"Absolutely," Mike added. Lisa felt warm around her cheeks and throat, avoiding Mike's eyes.

"It's good to have such an expert opinion," Rayburn sneered.

Lisa looked at Mike then and saw that he seemed murderously angry at Rayburn.

"That's enough, Jim," the deputy director said quietly. "What's your official objection?"

"His real objection," Mike intervened, "is that Dr. Heron's going to get a chance to experience, first-hand, the *equipment* fault in the capsule."

"Now, Mike," Gould objected, "that's not proven yet. Why don't you guys quit sniping at each other so we can get this show on the road?"

The deputy agreed, and finally Rayburn withdrew his objections. Lisa was embarrassed by the fuss, but at the same time she couldn't help loving Mike for his ardent defense of her, as well as his stubborn insistence on the fault being a technical one.

Lisa, it was concluded, would go into the simulator in the morning.

As the meeting broke up, she lingered a moment, hoping to have a private word with Mike. But Heinz was claiming her attention just as Gould was trying to hold Mike's. Their eyes met across the room; in Mike's Lisa could read frustrated apology, and she smiled at him in a reassuring way. His expression lightened, and he turned back to Gould.

It went that way for the rest of the day: not only was it necessary for Lisa to confer briefly again with a physician, who reminded her not to drink any alcohol, but she was also fitted for a suit and other equipment. She had to sandwich that in between her work with Heinz.

Somewhere in that hectic time she got a call from Mike. The racket in the background told her that he was in the engineering lab. He shouted over the noise, "I've got about thirty seconds. Please—don't leave without me this evening!"

"I won't!" she shouted back.

"Bless you!" he yelled, and hung up.

By five o'clock Lisa felt as if she'd been run through a winepress and had all her juice squeezed out. It was delightful to have a quiet interval completely alone; both Heinz and her secretary had left.

She went back to her desk, sat down and closed her eyes briefly. Then she heard a man's footstep in the outer office and got up to open her door.

He was standing there, staring at her with his emotions glowing in his eyes.

"I'm sorry." They said it together, almost as if they'd been rehearsed.

Suddenly it was comical; they both started to laugh. Lisa felt tears in her eyes, whether from laughter or sorrow she didn't know, or care. Maybe from both.

It was hardly a second before they were in each other's arms and she was feeling the hard splendor of his big body again, the wonderful shelter of his encircling arms, and he was saying softly, "Oh, Lisa, forgive me, I was such a damned fool. Let's never have another night like last night again."

She was murmuring, too, right in the midst of his pleading, "Oh, Mike, I was so foolish, so childish. I'm sorry."

"Well...now that that's taken care of," he whispered, and lowered his mouth to hers, his lips clinging, savoring, caressing the taste and shape and welcome of her mouth until she was dizzy with pleasure.

She leaned against his chest a moment, with the certain feeling that she'd been a long, long time away from home, and that now she was back again where she belonged. She told him that, her passionate words muffled against him. He held her more tightly, almost bruisingly tight, with his mouth against her hair.

Then he stepped back and said, "Let me look at you a minute. One of the greatest joys in my life has been just looking at you, Lisa. You're so beautiful."

His vivid glance took in her face and dress and hair, and he saw the glitter of his stars. "Stars in her eyes, stars at her ears," he murmured, grinning. "I think it's great that you're already dressed up for our celebration. I was afraid I'd have to start courting you all over again...hence my courting gear."

He made a mocking gesture at his summer dress uniform; he had the look of having just shaved and showered.

"Not likely, Colonel." She reached up and caressed his smooth jaw.

"Then let's get out of here, Doctor. I have some very special dinner reservations, made with undying hope and optimism at a very special place."

When they were driving toward Houston, she said, "Mike, I was very wrong last night and you were right. Adults stay and talk things out."

He reached out to touch her with one hand, his eyes still on the highway, and answered, "And I was wrong, too, and *you* were right. I'm a swell one to lecture anyone on being adult. It's going to be different now, Lisa, I swear to you." He put his hand back on the wheel and they drove on toward the city in contented silence.

When they drove onto lush, wooded grounds surrounding a luxurious Spanish-style hacienda, Lisa knew what Mike had meant by special. An attendant took the car after practically bowing them into an incredible interior.

"It's a replica of a sixteenth-century plantation in Mexico City," Mike said. Lisa could believe it; she almost expected Spanish grandees to enter the dining room in antique costumes. It was breathtaking.

Moreover, to her relief, the cuisine was European with Mexican overtones. She'd never developed a taste for hot Mexican food.

Mike seemed to read her when he watched her face light up as she looked over the menu. "I never figured you for a tamale freak," he declared. "This is just your kind of thing—subtle."

"You're wonderful. How do you know so much about me already?" she demanded tenderly.

"I got a lot out of Charlie early on," he confessed. "And I've got a whole dossier on you, lady. I wanted to find out as much as I could about the woman I love."

He raised his glass of club soda to her in salute, having passed up a cocktail in sympathy with her own alcohol ban for tomorrow.

"Mike Nesbitt, I think I'm happier at this moment than I've ever been in my life."

"So am I. But I promise, we haven't seen anything yet."

Their gazes held. She knew exactly what he meant. Despite all this grace and peace and loveliness, nothing could be quite so wonderful as being alone with him again and going into his arms.

The spell was unbroken when they left the magnificent restaurant. Lisa was almost floating as they got into the car and drove back to the hotel.

"At last, at last," he whispered, smiling at her with bright, sparkling eyes when he closed the door of the suite behind them. "Come here to me."

She looked up at him; his bright blue eyes were more wonderful than ever, with a depth that she hadn't seen in them before. It was as if their one-night separation had been a week or a month. She stepped into his arms and they closed around her. He was holding her against his body with such fierceness that she was aware of the straining of every muscle in his powerful frame.

She raised her face and he bent to kiss her, holding her ever closer; she felt her body flame.

When he released her, he whispered, "You see? We're meant to be together, Lisa. We're not meant to spend another night apart...not ever, ever again."

"I know, Mike. I know that now." Lisa raised her hands to his cheeks and stroked them, feeling him quiver at her touch.

"There are so many things I want to say to you." His eyes were pleading, tender.

"Not yet, my love. Not now." She smiled, tracing his lips with her fingers, caressing his stubborn chin, and she saw the blue eyes blaze with the same anticipation that pounded in her blood.

"Come. Come, my love." She lowered her hands from his head, letting her fingers trail over his broad shoulders and down his trembling arms.

Smiling, making a happy, wordless sound, he bent and scooped her up in his arms. "This is a very important ritual," he murmured, striding toward the bedroom, leaning over to kiss her half-parted mouth. She felt small, wavering tongues of fire raying out from her mouth to the dazzled flesh of her face and spread to her throat and breast; her arms and legs quaked, and she was dazed with her profound desire.

He stopped and kissed her again, gently at first, then with increasing savagery. Grasping her, he strode with longer, faster strides into the darkened bedroom. In the darkness he kissed her one more time before he put her on the bed.

He knelt over her, bending his head to hers, and their parted mouths clung. She closed her eyes to deeper blackness, exalted by his nearness, running her fingers up the length of his muscular arms, then down his torso, perceiving again the trembling of his body.

Now his hands explored the softness of her through the drifting fabric of her dress; one of her sleeves fell back, and he kissed the inside of her pulsing arm. She shivered and cried out. His hands stroked her sides with a passionate fervor, moving down to her waist and hips, down her legs until the hot touch was on her feet, sliding off her fragile sandals.

She heard the soft sound of them quietly striking the fuzzy carpet, felt his touch again on her sensitized feet, her ankles, her vibrant thighs. She sprang up, beginning to undress; he was trying to help, with awkward haste. But, laughing a little, she gently put his hands away and dealt with buttons and fastenings.

She scattered the clothes away from her and the cool air tickled her naked skin.

"Lisa, Lisa." His voice shook when his hands found her flesh, stroking her once more. "So smooth, so delicate," he said in a broken whisper. "I can't believe you. I can't believe *this,* Lisa."

Her name, spoken so softly in his southern fashion, had the slow, drawn-out sweetness of pouring honey, and she was as warmed by that sound as she was by the touch of his eager fingers. She felt an even more urgent trembling. A stronger heat overtook her, and she swayed inside his pleading grasp.

Suddenly Mike made a sound almost like someone in pain, and he threw off his clothes in what seemed hardly a moment until he was holding her again, their bare bodies pressed more closely than ever. She knew the absolute urgency of his desire and moved toward him until their bodies met in a wild, barbaric mating.

She gasped with her overpowering need, quivered with uncaring pleasure as their maddened bodies melded in a kind of primitive, unthinking dance. She could no longer tell her body from his, because now there was a madness between them such as she had never even dreamed of. Then there was no more consciousness at all, only the quickening, pounding rhythm of their frenzied motion, the slow, then less slow, quicker, quicker rising of unimagined pleasure.

Closer, closer, ever closer. They were utterly together as they drew toward the shimmering height. It was the only world there was, the only meaning. In the same breath, they cried out. She felt the power of his release, felt him almost recoil from a pleasure so huge and overwhelming that it seemed even his enormous strength could not support him. Every inch of him was shuddering, and she waited for her own mighty joy to ebb, but to her astonishment it still possessed her flesh, throbbing and vibrant in its infinite sweetness.

The trembling in his arms and body was decreasing and he held her to him, murmuring against her tumbled hair. Soon he was urging her to lie down on the soft, welcome width of the dim bed, lowering himself to lie beside her, drawing her close to him again until the naked length of their spent bodies matched and melded.

They lay that way for a measureless moment; she opened her mouth against the dampness of his chest, tasting the clean salt of his skin, feeling the slackened drum of his loud heartbeat against her face. His arm was like a warm, protective bond about her, his fingers splayed out against her naked roundness.

His hand moved slightly then, savoring her flesh that was relaxed to such softness that she could imagine it was hardly flesh at all, but only vapor. Her own wild heartbeat slowly eased; a long, pleased, shuddering sigh escaped her, and his skin prickled below her warm breath with evident titillation.

He raised his hand to her arm, to her shoulder, squeezing, asking her to move closer. She obeyed, burrowing her head into his chest; still silent, he kissed her hair. It was a long, long moment before they moved a little apart again.

Mike lay back and closed his eyes. In the faint light from the living room Lisa studied his face; she'd never seen it look this open or relaxed. He was smiling a childlike smile, broad and serene.

Lisa raised her hand, amazed at how boneless it felt, and traced his handsome profile. He smiled more widely, and murmured. When her fingers reached his lips, then his chin and throat, she could feel the vibration of his voice. She moved closer to him again, pressing her face into his neck, inhaling the scent of him with delight. He smelled like sunlight on fresh-planed wood.

Against his skin, she whispered to him of her love. He made an inchoate sound of utter happiness and began to kiss her. He drew her closer and closer to his body, with such a strong grip that she was completely captive. But that, she discovered, was just what she wanted to be right now. Already she felt her desire being reborn; new longing rose to take the first yearning's place.

And once again they were drawing together, as if they had never made love before and yet, also, as if they had never in all their lives at any moment been apart.

Lisa blinked as she came awake. Sunlight filtered through the ivory draperies. They had slept straight through the night.

She smiled and stretched out her arms, feeling marvelous. It had been ages since she'd slept so well. Turning her head, she saw that Mike was still deeply asleep. He was lying on his stomach with his long legs spread, in an apparent ecstasy of oblivion. She was tempted to pat him, but refrained, reluctant to disturb such pleasurable sleep.

Getting quietly out of bed, she retrieved their scattered clothes from the floor, grinning to herself and disposing of her things first. Mike's dress uniform was a wreck. She put his other things in a hamper, then gently smoothed the uniform over her bent arm. Then she put on her watch and checked the time—only seven. Well, she had a feeling that, for a Nesbitt, valet service would be available quickly and early.

She went into the living room and called, leaving the uniform spread out on the back of the couch. Then she crept back through the bedroom, showered and slipped on a robe. Mike was still asleep.

Now for some coffee, she decided. It would be lovely to linger over morning coffee and relive the night they had just shared. Then she remembered that today she'd be going in the simulator. Damn. That meant no caffeine, not even any vitamins. She'd have to order juice for herself and a big pot of coffee for

Mike, and just tough it out. She was sure that when she smelled coffee she'd react like an alcoholic around liquor. She had fervently echoed Mike when he had told her once that his blood stopped in his veins without morning coffee.

It would be a small sacrifice, though, she decided; it was going to be a very exciting day. She was in the midst of ordering when valet service arrived; how right she'd been. The staff snapped to, military fashion, for a visiting Nesbitt.

Waiting for their breakfast, such as it was, to arrive, she went back to the bedroom and slid the noiseless closet door open, debating what to wear. Looking out, she noticed that the sun had faded; it was overcast and heavy clouds were massing. She knew all about the famous Houston humidity, especially on an about-to-rain morning, so she returned to the closet and selected something cool.

She put a small folding umbrella into her big shoulder bag and slid the wonderful brown diamond studs into her ears.

After she'd received their order she saw that it was nearly seven-thirty so she resisted the impulse to sit and dream awhile. It was time to wake Mike up. She longed to share today's adventure with Charlie, and to call her father. But it was far too early to call New York; besides, she wasn't sure how her father would react to her entering the simulator, after that long-ago tragedy. It might worry him. Yes, it would be better, she resolved, to call him this evening after it was all a fait accompli.

She poured a cup of coffee; her mouth fairly watered at its scent. But she stiffened her backbone, drank the juice, sugared Mike's coffee and put it on the bed table. Then she sat down softly on the bed beside him and rubbed his back.

"Ummm," he said drowsily. "Nice." He turned his head toward her, blinking and smiling. "What's all this?"

"Reveille," she murmured, and kissed him.

Sleepy as he was, he returned her kiss ardently. Then he sat up, sighting the coffee. "Reveille, my royal American...elbow," he chuckled. "If it was really like this, there wouldn't be any civilians left."

She laughed and got up, sitting in the chair by the bed, watching him enjoy the first sip of coffee."

"Say, you didn't have any of this, did you?" His question was quick, anxious.

"No, I remembered," she reassured him. "But I'd kill for a cup of coffee right now. My head's already a little achy."

"Poor baby. Come here." She obeyed. "Sit down," he ordered. Very lightly he rubbed her brow and kissed it. "I wish that could cure it," he added softly. "Chin up. You'll be going in this morning, so by lunchtime you can drink coffee like crazy. We'll get you two pots."

She patted his face. "It's not so bad. It's better than five weeks without it, like those poor women who were tested."

"You've got that right." He finished his coffee almost apologetically and then threw back the sheet and jumped up. As always she reacted strongly to the sight of his splendid, tanned body.

"Oh, *my,*" she teased him, raising her brows.

"None of that, madam...or the simulator will be spinning around without a passenger." He strode off toward the shower.

While he was in it, his uniform was delivered, and Lisa hung it in the closet next to his other clothes.

"Where's my grubby uniform?" she heard him call through the half-open bathroom door. "You know, I've got another shirt, but those pants..."

"In the closet," she answered calmly. She wandered into the living room and sat down, hearing him open bureau drawers to find the fresh socks and underwear he kept on hand, then heard him exclaim, "Great!"

In a few minutes he strode into the room, grinning, dressed in his spanking-fresh uniform. "You're too good to be true, Lisa Heron." He was absurdly pleased by what seemed to her a small, insignificant thing, and her heart turned over with tenderness. He was so obviously unused to being cared for by a woman. In that moment she loved him more than ever.

She realized that she still hadn't said it; she still hadn't told Mike Nesbitt that she loved him. "Mike, oh, Mike," she said with a breathless fervor. "I love you. I love you so much. Do you know that?"

"Lisa." He stopped short, staring at her. "What did you say? Say that again."

"I love you, Mike," she repeated. With the saying of it, she knew that she must have felt this on that very first day, when she'd seen him on the terrace in the dazzling summer sun. Yes, even then, incredible as it might seem.

He seemed unable to say a single word. Still staring at her with amazement, he came toward her. At first he didn't take her in his arms. He merely enclosed her face with his shaky hands and just kept looking at her. Then with great gentleness he turned her face up to his and kissed her.

It was the lightest, most delicate of kisses. He said softly, "I'm almost afraid this isn't happening. I'm afraid you'll...disappear."

"It is happening. I won't disappear." She smiled up into his eyes.

"Oh, Lisa." Now he was holding her tightly, his big hands encircling her waist. "I thought you'd never say it, never feel it," he whispered.

For answer she moved more closely to him, kissing his neck below his ear, stroking his head with her hands. Time stopped for their profound and silent happiness.

But then, as she lowered one of her arms, she noticed what time it was. "Oh, dear," she said gently. "We've got to leave."

He sighed, automatically glancing at his own watch. "Yes," he agreed with reluctance, "I'm afraid you're right." Slowly he let go of her.

She smiled and patted his cheek. "We've got to get you some breakfast." It was understood that she'd have a special breakfast at the center.

"Not on your life. That would be cruel and inhuman treatment. I'll get something at the center later on." Mike grinned at her, but she knew he hardly realized what he was saying. His bright eyes looked dazed, almost drunk with excited happiness. He watched her fondly while she got her things together.

As they headed toward the center, Lisa thought the sun had never looked so golden or the city so utterly beautiful. Glancing up at Mike, she saw that he wore an expression of almost solemn happiness, and she reflected in silence, this is a commit. The term, meaning that a space mission was in inevitable motion forward, that there was no longer any turning back, made

Lisa's insides swoop and tremble. She felt a fateful apprehension merge with her joy. This was just like what it would be to step into a capsule, to be bound for the irreversible journey into space...this "commit" to the man beside her. But there was no other way. She should have known that from the beginning. Perhaps unconsciously she *had,* and that's why she'd been so reluctant.

They were silent as the miles unrolled behind them. He was the first to break it.

"How do you feel right now about going in?" he queried.

"Full of anticipation. I can't wait to experience it for myself." She smiled at his somber profile.

"You're great." He touched her briefly, then put his hand back on the steering wheel. "I just realized something—it's been a long time since you've mentioned a flight."

"A very long time. But I've had a few other things on my mind," she teased him. "So, Colonel, am I going to get one, do you think?"

"I'm working on it, Doctor. There's a possibility that Dr. Charlton may be dropping out of the program in October...family problems."

Family problems, Lisa repeated silently to herself. She wondered if Charlton had a daughter...like Charlie. And she remembered how completely she'd forgotten her own daughter.

"You know," Mike said abruptly, "I almost hate for you to get in that simulator. The pogo's pretty bad. But I love you for it, too. You've got more guts and brains than any woman I've ever known. And yet I want to...protect you from it. Understand?"

She did. She loved him for it. And putting her hand on his knee, she said so.

He looked relieved and very tender. "You're some lady, Lisa Heron."

He said that again to himself an hour later when he saw her coming into the lab in her small white g-suit with her name imprinted along the pocket, the American flag replica sewn on one shoulder. She looked so little, and so feisty, he thought, feeling his breath catch. Her feet were blunted and strange in the space boots; she was carrying her helmet under her arm.

She smiled at him and gave him a thumbs-up signal before she put the helmet on.

Then she entered the simulator as if it were something she did every morning of her life.

The hatch was secured.

Mike Nesbitt stepped to one of the portholes to observe.

She was lying on her back in a miniature cockpit, a biobelt around her to monitor her heart rate and body temperature; a small transmitter, connected to an electrode, was pasted over her heart.

All systems were go, and Mike swallowed, breathing shallowly.

Chapter 8

Lisa felt deeply excited but supremely confident. Three years ago she'd undergone tests far more grueling than this one promised to be—especially the centrifuge.

For that she'd sat in a small cabin mounted at the end of a centrifuge arm, which was sent spinning faster, ever faster, to increase the pressure of gravity. She'd felt an enormous force pressing her deeper and deeper into the chair, then had a sensation of being mashed; finally it had felt as if her lower body had swollen like a balloon.

Now, lying strapped with her feet higher than her head, it was totally different; in this simulated zero-gravity, up was down, and it was like lying on a couch. She was elated. Real blast-off would be just like this.

An airplane instrument panel was spread out overhead before her eyes; she'd been asked to take readings off the instrument panel while she did hand-eye coordination tests. They would gauge her alertness, mental acuity and response times throughout her time in the simulator. There was also a button she could push to ask to be released. But she wasn't about to do that before the set interval was up. Because this, she suspected, wasn't just a test run concerning the pogo—her performance here could also weigh heavily in their evaluation of her fitness for a flight.

The pressure was minimal at first; she felt slightly nauseated, but that passed. Calmly she gave her readings, speaking through a mike to the men outside. She was dimly aware of Mike's face peering into the porthole.

Then in the midst of giving her readings, she was suddenly overwhelmed with torpor. She fought the desire to drift into sleep. She willed her mind to alertness, her head aching from the lack of caffeine, pins and needles in her legs and feet.

She was grimly determined not to doze. She had to stay sharp.

Now she could feel a new sensation, a rather horrible one, all over her body. The simulator was vibrating so strongly that she could almost feel her teeth rattle. Her teeth, she thought, might break if they met. She opened her mouth wide, trying to control the trembling of her jaws.

That terrifying moment passed somehow, but now she heard the most terrible sound she'd ever heard in her life, one that was practically unimaginable. Her ears were pierced with a pain that was almost unendurable. It was as if she were listening to a weird, collective screaming, like the voices of a thousand souls in torment.

Her mind shouted, I want to get out of here! I need to get out of here!

But she held on grimly to her reason, willing her mind to shout back, it's an equipment fault. The fault's in the equipment, not in me!

Elated, almost weeping with relief, she could hear the horrible screaming voices soften slightly.

And then the weird pogo was going away just as mysteriously as it had come...just as her father had said it would.

Just as my father said...my father said...father said...The words she was thinking, or saying—she could no longer tell which—diminished as if spoken by someone moving farther and farther away.

And then she slept.

She opened her eyes. There was still an hour to go, and more than anything on earth she wanted to get out of this thing. She felt like screaming, like crying.

Not now, she resolved at once. Not now. Once again she willed herself slowly, gradually, to attain a kind of calm.

When she'd first wakened she'd thought that maybe they were right; maybe this thing had proven that she was unstable, that there was something wrong with her mind. Maybe a woman's emotions made her unfit for this; perhaps she had gone over the edge and would never return. How could she have imagined tormented souls, how could she have thought of hell, when this was only a machine?

But she summoned up all her courage and forced herself to think, to analyze. Her physical and mental health were beyond question. She'd undergone innumerable, rigorous tests to qualify not only for space flight but for her own profession.

The dreams, the hysteria, the exhaustion, the feeling of utter helplessness she'd suffered today, were because of an equipment fault acting on the body, the brain, the nervous system.

She knew that with a profound, intuitive knowledge that she realized was a genetic inheritance from her father, Philip Marley.

And she'd walk out of this thing straight and calm and smiling.

But at first, when it was over, she was afraid her legs weren't going to work. The hatch was open, and Mike was coming in to unstrap her; Gould and Rayburn were behind him.

She took off her helmet, giving them all a rather shaky smile.

"Are you okay?" Mike asked, his face anxious.

"I'm fine. Just fine." Her own voice sounded oddly loud in her ears, alternating with faintness as her ears popped a little. She shook her head.

Willing herself to walk steadily, she preceded the men from the simulator.

"So how was it?" Rayburn demanded.

Mike's face was like a thundercloud, but before he could speak Lisa answered evenly, "I'll write up a report at once. But not before I've had some coffee."

Mike chuckled, and Gould grinned, looking respectful.

"You heard the lady," Mike growled at Rayburn.

He led her into another room. She saw the two enormous urns of coffee and laughed out loud.

With the first sip she said to Mike, "Now my blood can circulate again."

In her own clothes again Lisa felt more like herself, and enormously proud of the quick transition she'd made from zero-g to normal. All the sleepiness and doubt were gone, and her mind was crystal clear as she dictated her careful, detailed report, then planned the next two days' testing with Dieter Heinz.

The report was done in time for the afternoon conference with Mike, Rayburn and the engineers. The latter were highly complimentary. Although Mike was discreetly quiet, he beamed.

"What's your opinion, Jim?" Gould asked Rayburn with an ironic inflection.

"I think the whole thing's garbage." Rayburn's answer was hard and cold.

"What the hell do you mean, Rayburn?" Mike's question cracked like a whip. Lisa fervently hoped he'd hold on to his famous temper.

"I mean it's ridiculous to test a *woman* in the simulator," Rayburn began hastily, "especially one who's your tool."

Lisa could hardly control her own fury, but she valiantly contained herself.

"This is a damned farce," Rayburn went on, staring at Mike. "Nesbitt will obviously go to any lengths to get his point across—including the seduction of the head psychiatrist."

Mike was on his feet now; Lisa noticed that he was almost white under his tan, and his eyes glinted dangerously.

"I've had it with you, Rayburn." He strode to Rayburn's chair and grabbed him by the collar, jerking him to his feet.

"Mike..." Gould warned, standing up. "Take it easy."

"Easy, hell!" Before Rayburn's guard could go up, Mike's fist shot out and caught the other man neatly on the point of his jaw. Rayburn fell to the carpet like an axed tree.

Lisa gasped. Gould swore softly, saying, "For Pete's sake, Mike...why in hell did you have to do that?"

Rayburn was getting to his knees, shaking his head dazedly, glaring at Mike Nesbitt. He drew himself up by holding the back of a chair, and muttered, "You'll pay for this, Nesbitt...you and your whole damned crew...*and* your girlfriend." Gould and another engineer were holding Mike by the arms.

Massaging his jaw, Rayburn added sourly, "I think the meeting stands adjourned." He walked a bit crookedly out the door and slammed it.

Lisa was trembling all over, mortified and shaken. As Gould and the other man let go of Mike, and Gould spoke to him in a low voice, she couldn't help remembering what Rayburn had said—that Mike would go to any lengths to get his point across. She herself had thought that, at the beginning.

Mike was coming toward her with a sheepish expression on his face. "Lisa, I..."

The door burst open and Mike's aide rushed in, calling out, "Excuse me, Colonel. There's an urgent call for you from the Johns Hopkins lab."

"Right." Mike gave her a pleading look, then followed his aide out of the room.

Lisa was in no mood to face Gould and the others. She got up and went out, too, closing the door gently behind her.

She hurried to Heinz's office and burst in on him.

"Good heavens, dear child! What on earth is the matter?"

Lisa sank down in a chair by his desk and poured out the whole thing. He nodded as he listened, looking somber.

"This is not too good," he agreed. "The obnoxious major will enjoy using this against you and Nesbitt, Lisa. It is appalling that he should say those things. But, as you know, he has always been opposed to women in space. How absurd." He repeated some things Gould had said about women's superiority in space, adding, "You eat less, weigh less, use less oxygen." He grinned. "With brains in addition, you have it all over us men. In space physical strength counts for nothing, as you know."

"I *do* know, Dieter. But what about the other thing—the emotional involvement?"

Heinz studied her. "Are you serious about this man, Lisa?"

"Yes." She realized once more how deeply true it was. She was committed to Mike Nesbitt, now and forever.

"Then you will overcome any difficulties," Heinz said confidently. "Rayburn is an embittered neurotic; I have been trying to get that across to the powers that be for the past two years. Is it not painfully obvious to you why he is so opposed to women being in the space program? Do you know his history?"

"No."

"He was engaged to a mission specialist...a pale copy of you. She rejected him for another man, a man as impulsive and—" he grinned "—troublesome as the dashing Nesbitt. So *much* antipathy toward you, my dear, can only mean Rayburn is highly attracted."

"Heaven forbid!" Lisa exploded. "I'm ashamed I didn't think of it myself."

"Why should you? You have always been unusually modest about your considerable charms. Rayburn is no doubt wildly jealous of Nesbitt...and to think that Nesbitt's team would be chosen for the flight just puts the candles on the cake, as they say."

"Icing on the cake," Lisa corrected, smiling. "Good heavens," she said, thinking of what Heinz had told her. "But Dieter, that *exhibition* of Mike's...I just..."

"Come, come, Lisa." Heinz chuckled. "You know young men are like that."

"But Mike's *forty*...and so am I," she protested.

"From where I sit, forty is nothing," Heinz retorted. "Besides, the fitness and ingenuity and daring required of those who go into space always make them seem younger than they are. Do I have to tell you that? What about your father?"

It was true. Her father had always seemed younger than he was. And she'd heard him talking about having some royal battles with his cronies. Yes, she'd made a mountain out of the smallest hill. She'd lived in New York so long that she was used to men suing instead of swinging when they lost their tempers. She laughed. "I guess you're right."

"Of course I'm right. What woman with blood in her veins can really object to a knight in shining armor fighting for her?" Heinz's laughter answered hers. "Now, as long as you're getting a free session, what is the latest news of your Charlie?"

"I haven't talked to her in days," Lisa admitted guiltily.

"Good. Let her simmer. She has your phone number."

"But she's going to the Cape Friday, and I have to be at the hotel when she comes for her things," Lisa said firmly.

"While I struggle along here without you?" Heinz demanded. "So that she will have another opportunity to reject you again? I think you are being a little masochistic, Lisa. And that, furthermore, you might be jealous of her father and that woman he's married to, yes?"

"Bett," Lisa said absently, weighing that. Was she jealous? She probably was.

"Ah, you see." Heinz patted her hand. "If I am being hard on you, it is what they term 'tough love.' It is not...what you use, too, on your patients, madam?"

Lisa had to laugh at his smug expression. "You've got me there, Dieter. Nevertheless, I must be there. I've got to try to reach her one more time."

Heinz shook his grizzled head as if he were a little exasperated at her obduracy.

There was a soft tap at the door. "Come, come," Heinz called out with impatience.

Mike came in, looking buoyant, without a trace of the chagrin he'd shown not long before. "Excuse me, please." He grinned at them as if the scuffle had never happened.

Heinz started to rise.

"Please, Heinz, don't go. This concerns you, too. I'd like to speak with you both, if you have a moment."

"Certainly." Heinz settled into his chair again.

"There's been a new development at the Johns Hopkins space lab—they've encountered pogo similar to ours in a simulator. The engineering staff favors our doing comparative tests and investigations there, *and* at Canaveral, Huntsville and Tullahoma. There's also something to check out in Pasadena. We've gotten the okay of the higher-ups to do so," Mike said.

"So...I assume that your 'investigations' will include psychological tests similar to those being done here?" Heinz guessed.

"Exactly. What I need is your permission, Doctor, for Lisa to use your new test methods. I understand," he said to Lisa, "that you're thoroughly familiar with them now."

She nodded. "Is this your way of telling me that I'm going on the road?" Her smile took the sting from her question.

"*Asking* you," Mike amended. Then he turned to Heinz. "Well, Doctor? Can we have your permission? The administrators would be most appreciative."

Heinz laughed. "In other words, this is an order, not a suggestion." His eyes twinkled with sardonic amusement.

"I wouldn't say that." Mike's lips twitched at the corners. "However, I've taken the liberty of having a statement typed up for you to sign, if you approve. The director wants to be quite sure that you're on record as the inventor of this test method, to protect you in the event of publication of results." He took a folded paper from his pocket, smoothed it out and handed it to Heinz.

"Well, well, you have thought of everything, Colonel." Heinz's sharp old eyes skimmed the statement. "Excellent. I see no reason not to sign." He did so decisively and handed the paper back to Mike. "And, furthermore, I see no reason why I cannot continue for a time without my excellent colleague." He darted a look at Lisa.

Men, she thought resentfully. Ten minutes ago he couldn't do without me for a few hours, but now he can dispense with me for an unspecified time. She knew from Heinz's expression that he was reading her, and her resentment faded. He's trying to protect me from myself as martyr-mother, she decided.

"When do we go?" she asked Mike calmly, and saw his bright eyes gleam with admiration and gratitude.

"Tomorrow morning, early."

Tomorrow. "That's...impossible."

"Why?" Mike demanded with consternation.

"Because Charlie's leaving Friday, and I've got to see her first," Lisa said quietly.

Slowly a bright flush stained his cheekbones. "Are you telling me that this whole project has to come to a standstill because of that?"

"Lisa..." Heinz interjected, as if he were correcting a disobedient child.

Heinz's tone and Mike's expression ignited Lisa's anger. How could either of them understand?

"Call her, Lisa," Mike said cajolingly, but she heard an edge of impatience in his tone.

She hesitated painfully, her instincts as a mother warring with her professional logic and detachment. She thought of all the difficult years, of women's struggles to establish themselves, all the old arguments from prejudiced men who claimed that they couldn't count on people who "ran home every time Willie had a cold"; the information that Gloria Charlton might have to drop out of the program because of family problems. And she remembered the days and hours with Charlie that she'd had to forgo to qualify as a psychiatrist. She was probably acting like a fool. Her daughter was seventeen years old, almost a woman. She would appear at the hotel on Friday, pick up her luggage and exhibit the same sullen lack of forgiveness she'd shown Lisa all along. And for that Lisa was supposed to hold up a whole project...endanger her career, and Mike's...possibly lose a flight in consequence?

No, damn it. She wasn't going to fall into Charlie's trap.

All these thoughts must have flashed through her mind in seconds, because it seemed as if no time at all had passed before she answered firmly, "You're right...both of you. I'll call her and get her things ready for her tonight."

"Now you're talking." Mike was buoyant again, and the look in his eyes was tender. Dieter Heinz was grinning from ear to ear.

"I'd better get back to town now," Lisa said in a businesslike way. "I have a lot of things to do."

She rose, and Heinz got up, too, kissing her on the cheek. "Bon voyage, my dear."

Almost before she could turn around, Mike had deposited her at the hotel and gone off on errands of his own. Lisa went up to her suite. As soon as she'd closed the door, she went directly to the phone.

At the ranch, Martha answered, saying Charlie was in the pool. "Could you please get her?" Lisa asked. "It's urgent."

After a bit of a wait she heard Charlie's brash, rather cool reply. "What's the emergency?"

Her indifference hurt. But Lisa made herself answer with as much warmth as she could. "Honey, I wanted to be here tomorrow when you came to collect your stuff. But we've got to fly out of town tomorrow to do some tests in a number of other places. I'm not sure right now how long it's going to take. But I'll have all your things packed for you. If you like I can leave them at the desk, or even send them on to the airport."

There was a brief silence.

"Charlie?"

"'We' is you and Mike, I take it." There was no mistaking the hot jealousy in her daughter's voice.

"Of course. This is really his project."

"And so," Charlie said resentfully, "he snaps his fingers and off you go, without even telling me goodbye."

The inconsistency of that almost maddened Lisa. Nevertheless, she said softly, "Honey, I *am* saying goodbye...now. This is the only time I'll have to do it. By tomorrow we could be in Tennessee or Florida or Alabama...even California. What's the matter with you, Charlie? In New York you were dying for me to get a flight; you urged me to come to Houston. Now you've done a hundred-and-eighty-degree turn. I just don't understand. Please...talk to me. Tell me what's happened to you. To us."

"Nothing's happened to *me*, Ma. You're the one that's changed. You're letting this guy use you, and you're loving it. When you look at me you don't even see me."

Lisa was perversely encouraged by Charlie's tone. At least she was reaching her, in a way. "Honey, I *always* see you." Then she thought of the other thing Charlie had said. "What did you mean, Mike's using me? Where did you get that idea?"

"I met a girl whose uncle is a bigwig at the center. She said everybody knows about Mike Nesbitt and his maneuvers."

Lisa began to see. "What's her name?"

"What difference does it make? Her name's Helen Rayburn. Her uncle knows everything that goes on."

"I see." Indeed she did. "For your information, Charlie, James Rayburn is a liar, and—"

"I don't believe it, Ma," Charlie cut in. "Look, what are you going to do with my stuff? Deliver it to the airport, or leave it at the desk?"

That did it. "Since you didn't show me the courtesy of telling me when your flight is, I'll leave it at the desk," Lisa snapped before she could control herself.

"Fine. Be seeing you...sometime."

To Lisa's consternation Charlie abruptly hung up. Now she was in a confused state of pain and anger. Damn Rayburn and his manipulative lies, she reflected savagely. Turning her own daughter against her...and Mike. And heaven knew what Martha Harris must be thinking about Lisa's depositing her daughter there all this time. Well, that was the least of it, of course. The worst was the abrupt and angry goodbye.

But she had no time to brood; there was too much to do right now. She replaced the receiver, which she'd been absently holding, and took her bag off her shoulder.

She took out the hastily scribbled itinerary that Mike had given her in the car. Baltimore tomorrow, she noted, then Tennessee, Alabama, California. They'd be spending two or three days, depending on what happened, in each location.

As best she could she packed lightly yet managed to cover all the bases. Lovingly, and last, she examined the velvet case of stars and studs; she transferred them all to a traveling jewel case. She was resolved not to be without them.

The very sight of them recalled Mike so vividly that she felt her heartbeat quicken. He was unique, fantastic. Suddenly the idea of traveling with him, alone, was such a delight that it blotted out the unpleasant conversation with Charlie, like sunlight driving away shadow.

She felt so much better that when she packed Charlie's things she managed without dissolving into melancholy, as she had feared she would. Everything would be all right, she determined; it would *have* to be. She'd sit down right this minute and begin a long letter to her daughter, and mail it to the Cape tomorrow morning so it would be there when Charlie arrived.

It would express everything she'd been unable to express in person: her unchanging love and loyalty to Charlie; the happiness that Mike offered; all the exciting happenings at the center. She'd even include a joking reference to Greg, reminding Charlie of that particular silver lining...and of course a happy paragraph or two about Philip Marley's part in all this and his improving condition. Surely her daughter, who adored her grandfather, would be moved by that.

Lisa sat down at the hotel desk and began to write. She was so absorbed that the buzz of the phone made her jump.

It was Mike. "Hi, darling. Did you get Charlie?"

"Yes. But I'm afraid it wasn't a very inspiring conversation," Lisa admitted. However, she didn't want to whine about it, so she made her answer purposely ironic.

"Well, you sound great." He was obviously pleased by that. "It'll work out. You'll see."

"Of course it will. Where are you?"

There was a loud, exasperated sigh. "At the center again, and up to my...eyebrows in about two hundred problems. That scrubs dinner, I'm afraid. I'm sorry about that, darling."

She reassured him, saying she had plenty to keep herself occupied.

"This may run so late," he went on, "that I won't be able to get back there until the wee hours. I'm not too crazy about that, as you must know," he chuckled.

"Neither am I. But we're going to be leaving practically at dawn, so I'll welcome the sleep. Besides, this isn't the last night in the world now, is it?"

"You bet it's not," he said fervently. "We're going to have lots of lovely nights in the next couple of weeks, Lisa Heron."

"I can't wait, Mike. I miss you already," she said, meaning it very much.

"Damn, I miss you, too. But I've got to go now. If worse comes to absolute worse, I'll see you in the morning at the hotel."

She hung up softly, realizing how hungry she was. She ordered dinner in her room and enjoyed it with a whole new appetite.

She finished her letter to Charlie, then sealed and stamped it for mailing. Her spirits rose. This would be the first step toward winning her daughter back, to reassuring her that nothing could destroy their love and closeness. She'd send her cards and letters from everywhere along the route, and maybe find some gifts she would like, as well.

By the time she was ready for bed, Lisa was looking forward to the next day eagerly. She and Mike would be starting off on the first adventure that could truly be called their own.

Mike raised his cocktail, saluting Lisa. In the candlelight his eyes glimmered more brightly than the pale liquid in his glass. She raised her wineglass to him.

"I've already toasted you," he said, "as my colleague. How about another one, for how beautiful you are?"

She smiled in answer, and they touched glasses, then sipped. She set her glass down on the pink linen tablecloth, delighting in the fresh pink roses on their table, exactly matching the cloth. Reece's Downtown in Baltimore was a beautiful restaurant, and she felt extremely festive, anticipating their Chicken Narcissus, described as breast of chicken with honey and Mandarin liqueur.

Mike had an encyclopedic knowledge of good restaurants, she'd discovered, and a positive genius for creating a festive atmosphere. He'd said they deserved to celebrate that night, and she had to agree—they'd been going at it hard since the morning before.

Their flight had put them in Baltimore at the start of the business day; after checking into the hotel they'd plunged at once into their business at the space lab, where Lisa had conferred with the local psychiatric team and Mike had been deep in engineering and administrative matters all day. Then the night before they had fallen asleep very early, after a splendid dinner at another delightful place called the Bronze Elephant.

The old building in which the restaurant was housed had once been both the home and showroom of a family of furniture makers, and the diners could still enjoy the hand-carved woodwork and other handcrafted things. Lisa had played tourist, sending Charlie one of the restaurant's postcards. She had scribbled, "Bronze elephants are even slower to forget the ones they love."

This morning Mike and Lisa had awakened very early, wild for each other, uniting with a wondrous freshness and joy. All day she had glowed with the aftermath and, inspired, had been able to get through an enormous amount of work. As of now, she was confident that the testing procedures she'd helped set up were faultless. Mike was gratified with the results of his meetings, too. "It begins to look like your father's solution is the one," he had told her.

After they had eaten and were lingering over coffee, Mike surveyed Lisa. "You look more like April than July," he murmured. She was wearing a thin dress the color of new leaves, with the diamond stars and chartreuse peridots in her ears. "It's like a steam bath out there. Where to, lady? Shall we take a boat ride?"

"I vote for hiding in air-conditioned splendor," she said.

He answered that with a significant grin, knowing she meant their hotel. They returned, and while he went over his day's notes Lisa reviewed hers, then wrote to her father and sent another postcard to Charlie. It was a close, companionable, lazy evening. They both looked forward to the next day, Sunday, which would give them a welcome break. Mike had business in Washington Monday morning, so they agreed to leave late the next morning.

They arrived in Washington in time for lunch. Mike, with his usual expertise, had checked them into a famous hotel that had its own equally famous restaurant, combining sixteenth-century Spanish decor with the flavor of old Georgetown. Wood paneling from venerable barns added a unique touch.

The weather had turned cooperative; it was unseasonably cool, so they decided to take a long walk after lunch. En route to the museums, they passed a prestigious department store whose windows were already displaying autumn finery.

"Hey, look at that," Mike said and stopped. A mannequin stood alone in the window, dressed in a soft, elegant suit of winter white, with a matching cowl-neck blouse, white beret and strings of fake pearls. "You'd look gorgeous in that," Mike commented, grinning at Lisa.

"It *is* lovely." But her own attention was captured by a vivid red-and-blue ensemble displayed on a teenage-size mannequin. "Now that's Charlie," she remarked. "Only a size four could get away with that."

"You know, it is." Mike sounded thoughtful, even mysterious.

They walked on, glorying in the miraculous coolness, and spent a pleasant hour or so around the museum area.

It wasn't until the next afternoon, when they were getting ready to fly to Canaveral, that Lisa realized what had been behind Mike's mysterious tone.

He was pacing the carpet restlessly. "What's the matter?" she asked. "We're all squared away. Did something go wrong at your meeting? I thought you said it went well."

"Oh, it did." His voice had an edge of annoyance. "But we're not quite squared away."

Before Lisa could ask him what he meant, there was a knock at the door, and he rushed to open it. A hotel attendant was standing on the threshold with a huge box.

"Finally!" Mike exclaimed. He tipped the man and took the box, bringing it jubilantly to Lisa.

"What on earth...?" She smiled at his triumphant manner, unwrapped the box and gasped.

The entire outfit that Mike had so admired was in the package—suit, blouse, pearls and beret; even gloves, bag and shoes. "Mike," she said. The one word expressed her pleasure, her mingled reproach and astonishment. "You're too much, darling."

"I'm just enough for you, lady," he retorted.

"Mike...the other window. You didn't..."

He laughed. "I did. Why not? All those things were cute, and you did say they were Charlie. They're on their way."

She hugged him close. "Oh, Mike. But how did you get her address?" He chuckled. "Of course," she answered herself. "The postcards."

"Got it the first time, Doctor. Now, you'd better pack those things, too, or we're going to miss that plane."

She did, and all the way to the airport, and while they were on the plane, Lisa reflected on his wild impulse, his imaginative generosity. He had the talent for making everything seem like a fairy tale; more than anyone she'd ever known, he had so much fun with money. It was an endearing quality, and she had the conviction that life with him would always be one big Christmas surprise.

He did things so expertly, too, that it amazed her. He'd known her size from conferring with the center about her spacesuit, and had remembered Charlie's from Lisa's single absentminded comment outside the store window.

When they touched down at Canaveral, Lisa felt a great nostalgia. The small "space hamlet" in Central Florida had been little more than a mosquito-ridden swamp when she was a small child.

Lisa mentioned that to Mike, and he smiled. "There wasn't much enthusiasm here for a while, but they'll be planning the next shuttle party for October."

Launchings had always been a big tourist attraction, and local businesses had built their profits around them. These days launching parties had become shuttle parties, to keep up to date.

Later in the day, after they'd conferred at the space center, Mike was a little less buoyant. "I hope they'll be having shuttle parties," he confided to Lisa. "This damned pogo is almost an epidemic—Baltimore, and now Canaveral. And on top of that I got some static about your father's theory from these jerks. I've got to have a long talk with Mr. Marley tonight."

They both did, and Mike was reassured by the conversation. "I thought I was a hotshot engineer," he told Lisa, "but Phil Marley is the greatest thing since von Braun."

Lisa was bursting with pride, elated throughout the rest of their stay, and her high spirits continued through the trips to Huntsville, Alabama and Tullahoma, Tennessee.

Now they were on the last leg of their journey, to Pasadena, California. As the huge jet winged westward she reviewed the past days as they related to her father and Charlie. Every time she'd spoken to her father, he'd sounded better and better. The last time he'd told her that his release might come as early as September. Late at night, she'd written him page after page of detailed reports on her work in the program. She felt that the letters might be aiding his recovery. And she knew the active part he was playing by conferring with Mike was the most important of all.

As for Charlie—Lisa had bombarded her with postcards from everywhere, souvenirs of Canaveral and a couple of letters written in affectionate travelogue fashion with hardly a mention of Mike. She'd called her several times, as well; twice Charlie was out, and the third time, when Lisa had reached her, the marvelous package from Washington had not yet arrived. Surely, Lisa decided, Mike's generous gesture would have to have *some* softening effect...unless, heaven forbid, Charlie thought he might be trying to buy her.

She dismissed the gloomy thought, resolving to hope for the best. Charlie had sounded much warmer on the phone the last time they had spoken.

Besides, Lisa said to herself, glancing aside at Mike in the neighboring seat, we'll *have* to work it out. There was no turning back for her now: Mike Nesbitt was a definite "commit."

"We've covered a lot of ground...literally and figuratively." Mike's eyes met Lisa's in the casual, dimly lit restaurant in Pasadena; it was their last night before they went back to Houston. "Tired?"

"Nice tired," she said, feeling utterly relaxed and happy. Their surroundings were easy and homelike; a serene turn-of-the-century ambience had been created. "The tired of having accomplished something."

"That's exactly the way I feel," he said companionably. "You know, I was feeling pretty down about the situation in Canaveral and Tullahoma. But Huntsville and Pasadena brought things back into perspective, wrapped it up. And you know, darling, it's mostly because of your father...and because of you."

He reached across the table, lifted her hand and brought it to his lips. She was overwhelmed by emotion—tenderness and excitement and gratitude, pride in and love for her father.

"What gets me," Mike said, still holding her hand against his cheek, "is the way I can say about three words to him on the phone, and in seconds he's come up with something new and better than before." He pressed her hand, and she delighted in the feel of his tough, smooth skin, his hard jaw under her fingers. "It's more obvious than ever where you got your brains, Doctor."

"Thank you kindly, Colonel." He released her hand with another light kiss, but still held it across the table. "And you're brilliant, too."

His eyes admired her. "You're beginning to look like a surfer, you know." She had gotten a deeper tan in just the few days they'd been in California; they'd managed quite a bit of sea and sun in the midst of their other activities. "You're always so lovely, Lisa," he said softly. "I still can't quite believe it. You've actually told me three times on this trip," he said teasingly, "that you love me."

She thought, he tells me every day. "And I'll tell you three more times right now. I love you, I love you, I love you, Mike Nesbitt."

"Then don't you think," he asked with deceptive lightness, "it's time we got married?"

Her pulses quickened, and she felt a warmth suffuse her body. "Oh, Mike."

"Surely it doesn't come as a great surprise?" he teased her gently. Then he sobered and studied her expression. "Lisa?"

"No, darling. No. it's no surprise. It's...beautiful." She was thinking, this is what I've really wanted all along, and I just couldn't admit it to myself. And here I am hedging, hesitating. There was only one reason for that—Charlie. How would she react if she was abruptly presented with Mike Nesbitt as a stepfather?

"'Beautiful' is nice, honey, but it's not yes." Mike looked anxious, but his tone was still soft, coaxing. "*Is* it yes?"

She hesitated only an instant before she said, "Yes, Mike. It is." Charlie was just going to have to accept it.

His eyes lit up as if they were blue fire, and a wide smile split his tanned face, revealing the dazzling white of his teeth in contrast to the darkness of his weathered skin. He took a quick, ragged breath, still holding on to her hand. "I was speechless there for a minute," he laughed. "It was like being pitched into zero-gravity without a helmet. Did I hear you right...? Did you actually say yes?"

"Yes, yes," she repeated, grinning. "You heard me."

"Oh...Lisa. When? Tomorrow?"

She laughed at his question. "Tomorrow we fly back to Houston."

"Don't remind me." There was a peculiar shadow in his eyes. "For years I've been obsessed with space flight, with my work. Now for the first time in my whole life I just want to forget everything, to be alone in the world with you."

"I know, Mike, I know. Right this minute that sounds like heaven," Lisa said wistfully. "To quit pushing, driving...forget all my responsibilities, think of absolutely nothing but you." She smiled at him, and his hard hand slid up her arm, sending delicious shudders along her body.

"And we can't. Not now, when they're champing at the bit in Houston, and the project's at its most critical stage. But as soon as this thing is wrapped up—and we're so *close* now, Lisa—you'll marry me. Won't you, darling?'' He looked anxious all over again.

''Yes, Mike. Oh, yes.'' She realized that she wanted that more than she'd ever wanted anything. To be away from him, even for a single night, was unimaginable now. ''But first,'' she added with slow reluctance, ''I've got to get things straight with my daughter.''

His smile died, and his lips tightened. But he said quietly, ''You haven't said much about Charlie since we left Houston, Lisa. How did she sound when you spoke to her?''

''Thawing a bit, I think,'' Lisa answered, feeling uncertain, almost wishing she hadn't brought the issue up. But she had to; the problem wasn't going to go away because they ignored it. ''Heinz told me,'' she confided, ''that I can't let her run my life.''

''Our lives,'' he corrected. ''He's right. I'm not going to have to ask her permission, am I, Lisa?'' His grin was crooked. ''Surely I don't even need your father's okay, not at this stage of the game. I certainly hadn't counted on having to ask Charlie.''

Although he was smiling, there was a sharpness in his question that disturbed her a little.

When she didn't answer, he went on urgently, ''You know, Charlie will be going away someday...but I'll be here forever.'' His hard fingers closed around her wrist, and her pulses drummed at the commanding touch.

''I think that's what I hoped you'd say from the very beginning.'' She put her other hand over his and stroked it. ''And I think we've talked about it enough for now. Let's start forgetting, Mike. We have tonight, and tomorrow.''

"Blessed Sunday. Consider everything forgotten...except you and me." He asked for the check. "And speaking of tonight—I hope you'll like the place I've chosen. I thought it would be easier on you to be near Cal Tech, we've been working such long hours. But now we can have our getaway."

He paid the bill, and they walked out of the restaurant and got in the car. He turned and checked the back seat. "There it is, right on schedule."

She looked, too. Their packed suitcases were there.

He laughed at her surprised expression. "Even as we lolled at dinner, all our gear was being stowed away. So off we go."

It was marvelous, she thought, his quick, sweeping way of handling every last detail. "I like the way you do things, Colonel."

"I like the way *you* do things, Doctor. Especially this." He took her in his arms and slowly bent his head to hers, finding her willing mouth with his. His lips were warm and eager and demanding. She let herself go into that headlong fall, that wavering submission. Always, when he kissed her, held her, drew her so close to his big, hard body, it was like a sudden, sweet immersion into zero-gravity.

He let her go with quickened breath and great reluctance. "We have miles to go before we...meet," he whispered.

Then they were driving off swiftly toward the coast.

Chapter 9

"It's beautiful," she breathed when they stopped outside a white beach house high on the palisade. There was a panoramic view of the curving shore of the Pacific by the brilliant light of the moon.

"And no one's home but us," he said softly. "I had the welcome lamps put on." He indicated the golden illumination that streamed from several windows of the house. "Gold for Lisa." Their gazes held for an instant. Then he asked, "Shall we go down to the beach for a while?"

She nodded.

They got out, and he led her to a flight of stairs descending to the moon-paled sand, and then with clasped hands they wandered along the beach.

Suddenly he stopped, stooped down before her and took off her sandals, tossing them away. He bared his own feet, then took her hand again, and they continued their slow progress across the warm sand. Now there was literally no one else in the world, she reflected, and she felt that they were moving hand in hand through the strange, pale light of an alien planet, their dazzled bodies becoming accustomed to the foreign weight of unknown air.

He was a maker of magic for her; he had cast his spell over her mind and senses. Now there was only this drifting into empty space; the silver light was shining not from the moon orbiting the familiar planet earth, but from one of the odd moons of another galaxy, where the motion of the planets was honey-slow.

Mesmerized by his closeness, the silvery light and the wondrous silence broken only by the sighing of the sea, she recognized that he, too, was bemused by the same lovely strangeness that baffled her. Turning, he looked down into her face, and his vivid eyes were glazed with wonder and emotion.

Swiftly he let go of her hand and, grasping her about the waist, pulled her roughly, with great urging, to his body, capturing her in his muscular arms, holding her so near that she was immediately aware of his towering need, his trembling excitement. With an excruciating, stately motion, he lowered his head and took her mouth.

Her nerves were electrified; her senses whirled like the bright stream of light from a comet. Her shuddering mouth pressed his in answer, and her shaky hands found themselves caressing his head, his neck, his shoulders. All the while his own hard fingers explored the curves and softness of her vibrant flesh.

There were no words between them. He raised his hands to her back and unfastened her sundress, letting it fall to the sand.

He took an unsteady step backward and looked at her, his gaze a cool fire in the pallor of the moon's light, and she knew that where she had been golden in the sun she was now all silver. He knelt and peeled away her small bikini of shiny satin.

When he stood up again and began to unbutton his shirt, she stopped him with a tender, smiling gesture. She unbuttoned his shirt herself and slipped it from his body.

She stroked his bare chest with her quickening touch, and he made a sound of delight, ridding himself of the rest of his clothes until, unfettered, they were once more pressed together, her lips on his neck and his mouth against her hair.

Slowly he urged her with his touch down to the warm and powdery sand where he spread her dress out beneath her. She lay back in the dazzling brightness of the argent light and looked up at him as he kneeled above her, overwhelmed and dizzied by the love and worship on his face in that moment before their bodies were joined.

"I haven't reentered," Mike admitted early on Monday morning when they walked into the lobby of the Golden Seasons.

"Neither have I. I wonder when I will." Lisa gave him a tender look, still heavy with the languor of the last two nights and the perfect day between. On that magical night at the beach, after they had finally come to their senses again, they had raced into the surf for a playful swim. Then, chilled, they had gathered up their things and raced up the stairs to the house. Mike had wrapped them both in gigantic towels and gone to retrieve their things from the car.

Later they had eaten ravenously again, slept deeply and awakened to a sweet, slow interlude of love. Sunday had been a golden interim of drowsy tenderness, of sea and sun. It seemed to Lisa that hardly an hour had passed before they had boarded a jet in Los Angeles for an early flight to Houston.

"I'm still on the beach," she murmured when they stopped at the desk to check for messages. Lisa was glad that there were none. They were heading for the elevator bank when the desk clerk answered a phone and called out, "Dr. Heron!"

She stopped and went back to the desk. "An urgent call for you, from New York. I'll have it transferred to the third house phone, right over there."

Lisa excused herself to Mike and went to the indicated phone.

"I'm glad I finally got you." It was Jack. "I've been chasing you all over California, missing you everywhere."

"What is it?" she asked with apprehension.

"Charlie's disappeared."

Her heart fluttered in her throat. "What?"

"She ran away." Jack sounded exhausted. "She's been gone since Saturday night."

An awful hysteria overtook Lisa, and she asked sharply, "But my God, why? What happened? You're in New York.... Does that mean you think she's there?"

"Calm down, Lisa. I'm just as worried as you are. First of all, nothing really happened. She seemed perfectly okay. She and some friends went out Saturday night, and they brought her home about one-thirty. Bett and I went back to sleep, and then yesterday morning she was gone. Her bed hadn't been slept in."

"But where have you checked? Did you—"

"I told you, Lisa, let me tell it." Her ex-husband sounded exasperated now as well as deeply tired. Out of the corner of her eye, Lisa saw Mike approaching.

She barely noticed when he reached her and put his hand on her shoulder, she was listening so intently. "I didn't want to call you until we'd had a chance to check things out," Jack went on. "She took Bett's car, and when we checked the airport, it was there. They said someone of Charlie's description had bought a ticket to New York."

"But..."

"Wait, wait," Jack said irritably. "I came down yesterday; of course the first place I looked was your house. Nothing doing. Brenda hadn't heard a word from her. I called your mother on the Island." Hearing Lisa's gasp, he said quickly, "Don't worry, I didn't tell her anything yet. Just pretended I was saying hello. When she asked me how Charlie was enjoying the Cape, I knew right away she hadn't heard anything, either."

"Well, thanks for handling it that way, Jack," Lisa said miserably.

He continued. "Naturally I checked out all her friends, but so far I've come up with zilch. The police wouldn't do anything until she's been gone for twenty-four hours, but they're starting to work on it today. However, I don't have to tell you how many teenage runaways there are now...or how pessimistic the police are in consequence. Anyhow, I've hired a private detective, too. And, Lisa, I figure that among ourselves we can come up with a likely place...based on her interests, things like that."

Lisa saw that Mike had drawn back a bit and was waiting with a serious expression. She gathered that he'd understood the direction of the conversation.

"We'll find her, Lisa," Jack resumed doggedly. "I don't have to tell you how rotten I feel.... I mean, she was staying with us and all that, but..." His voice trailed away.

"But she's not a child," Lisa said firmly. "You can't be *that* responsible for her, Jack. Look, I'll find out when the next plane leaves for New York...."

She saw Mike stiffen.

"No, no," Jack responded hastily. "That's exactly the reason I called you; to tell you that you don't have to come here. I think I've got it all nailed down as much as possible. When I talked to your mother she told me you're up to your ears in the project there in Houston. I'll keep you posted all the time."

Lisa debated. Then, noticing Mike's expression, she said, "Well, let me sleep on it. Do you have my number at the center?"

"Sure. I got it from Brenda."

After a few more questions on her part, and assurances on his, Jack hung up.

Lisa replaced the receiver dully and stood there looking at Mike.

"Honey, honey, please don't look like that." He took her in his arms, oblivious of everyone around them, drawing her head down to his chest.

"You heard what it was about," she murmured against him. She raised her head as he nodded, and bent to pick up her big tote bag.

"I'll take that." Mike relieved her of it and made a sign to the waiting bellboy, motioning toward the elevator. Lisa and Mike preceded him into its baroque, wood-paneled interior, making the ascent in heavy silence.

When they were alone again in the suite, Mike said, "Come here, baby. Sit down." He took her by the hand and walked her to the long couch. "I've asked them to send up some coffee. You look like you need it."

Lisa sank down on the soft, pale couch and leaned her head back. "I do. Thanks."

He sat down close to her and smoothed her hair back from her brow. "So...I take it Charlie's done a disappearing act. I'm sorry, honey. Tell me what your ex said. I assume that was him; I heard you call him Jack."

"Yes. Sorry you had to get it in bits and pieces. I was just too..."

"Forget it. Tell me what happened." He patted her cheek.

In the midst of everything she couldn't help reacting to the gesture. She rubbed her face against his hand like a cat. Then she took a deep breath and repeated what Jack had told her.

"Well," he said encouragingly, "it sounds like he's done all right. He's got a handle on it. Doesn't sound like you need to go to New York right now."

She didn't answer, thinking, what he's saying is that he hopes I won't go, that I won't leave him. Just then room service arrived with the coffee, and watching him go to the door, Lisa reflected that she didn't want to leave him. Right then she almost wished she didn't have a child.

She felt an instant rush of guilt. How could she think like that? While she had been enjoying herself with Mike, while they had been experiencing their magical weekend in California, her own daughter had run off in misery and confusion. She didn't even know where Charlie was; she might be hurt or sick, or...No, she couldn't even think that word.

"Here." Mike was serving her as gently as if she were a child. He poured her a cup of black coffee and handed it to her. "Drink this. You look pretty upset, Lisa."

She drank the coffee and felt a little better. "I'll be all right as soon as I get my bearings. I feel a little like someone who's been hit over the head," she said wryly.

"You're not alone." He sighed and poured some coffee for himself, joining her on the couch. "Talk about reentry," he commented. "Straight from sunny California to catastrophe, without even one hour of reorientation."

"Oh, Mike, I know. It was so...beautiful." She stroked his hand. "Then to be hit with this.... I'm frantic about her."

"Try not to be. She's a smart, citywise kid. She'll be fine." Lisa couldn't prevent a twinge of resentment at his tone. There it was again: he really didn't understand. He couldn't.

She was forming a reply when he said, with the same disturbing lightness, "Look, I've got to make some phone calls. Do you want to take it easy awhile, then come out to the center later on in the copter?"

She shook her head. "No. Thanks, but I think work will be the best medicine today. Make your calls and I'll unpack."

"I'm glad to hear you say that, honey. We're at a very critical stage now. I'm sure they'll want those test reports from you today. Fine." He stood up and went to the phone.

Lisa had their cases unpacked and their things put away by the time he was ready to leave. She changed her dress quickly. Her briefcase was already in perfect order, so they lost no time in getting to the center.

The whole day went by like lightning, but despite the pressures of work, Charlie was constantly on her mind. The engineers were mapping out a whole new procedure, and Mike got so involved that he didn't get back to the hotel until late that night. Earlier Lisa had debated about calling Jack again, but had decided there was no point; she knew he'd call her at once with any news.

Tuesday was almost a replay of the day before. Rayburn, Lisa noticed thankfully, was rarely in evidence. Aside from a nasty reference to "junkets," he hadn't had much to say to her or Mike. She wondered what was going on and marveled that the fight between Mike and Rayburn seemed to have been totally forgotten. Mike told her that he'd have to stay overnight at the center; they'd struck a snag in their research.

It hurt her that he'd been so preoccupied that he'd barely mentioned Charlie to her, but she had to admit that the project had reached such a critical stage that it was understandable. Nevertheless, on Tuesday night she called Jack. Even if it was a futile gesture, she had to make it. He still had nothing to report, and now her anxiety had become utter terror.

By Wednesday evening, having slept little and worked very hard, she was in a pitiable state of nerves. Mike, too, was exhausted; he told her that he'd slept only about two hours the night before. They were both dead on their feet by the end of dinner.

When they got back to the suite, Mike shut the door with a decisive air, as if he were shutting out the world and all responsibility. "Sweet rest...sweet you," he said drowsily to her, taking her in his arms. They felt lax and heavy on her body.

She dreaded having to tell him what she'd decided: that she had to fly to New York on Friday. It would be utterly impossible to do so tomorrow—she had such a load of unfinished work that even getting it all done by Friday seemed a superhuman task. But she would. She had to.

"Mike..."

"In a minute, darling." He seemed savagely impatient in his weariness. "I'd like to shower. Unless you want to first."

"No, no. Go ahead."

He was halfway to the bedroom as she said it.

By the time she'd finished bathing he was already half asleep.

She padded to the bed and got in beside him.

"Umm..." With closed eyes he drew her to him.

"Mike? Darling..."

"Um?" He frowned a little. She wondered if she should wait to tell him. Better not, she resolved. She didn't want to spring it on him tomorrow when he'd be intent on work.

"Darling, I've got something to tell you," she whispered.

There was a flicker of the golden brown lashes, and she could see a trace of bright blue irises when he came to attention. "Can't it wait, darling? I'm beat." His words were thick.

She realized that she'd waited until the worst possible time and decided she'd better postpone it. "Sure." She turned out the light, and he rolled over to take her into his arms, snuggling against her.

Lisa lay awake stiffly, knowing she wouldn't be able to fall asleep, but reluctant to disturb the weary man beside her. Nevertheless, she made some restless motions, without volition.

Finally he mumbled, "Lisa? Can't you sleep?"

"No," she admitted, stroking the big arm around her waist.

He sighed. "What is it?"

"I'm sorry I woke you. Please go back to sleep."

"You know I can't do that, Lisa, when you're lying awake worrying." He spoke gently, and his words were clearer. "I'm up now anyway." He slid his arm from under her and sat up in bed to get a cigarette, snapping on the lamp by his side of the bed. He turned to smile at her. "Now we have some light on the subject."

She was full of self-reproach when she saw how tired he looked; there were shadows under his eyes, and sharp lines extended from the corners of his nose to the edges of his lips.

"This is awful," she said. "Waking you like this."

"Come on now, lady. How can I snore away like a swine when you're awake and anxious?" He grinned tiredly at her, blinking away the smoke.

Her heart melted within her. He was so sweet, so considerate, always so touchingly eager to be close to her. "Darling, I think I'd better fly to New York Friday."

"Friday! How can you, honey, when you've got a week's worth of work to get through? It's impossible," he protested.

"Not for me," she said stubbornly. "If I go in early tomorrow and keep at it until late, I can wrap up enough so that Heinz can take over. Even I can't understand my handwriting," she joked, trying to lighten the moment, "but fortunately I've got a lot of stuff on tape, so it's no problem."

"And what if someone misinterprets a word here and there? Tapes aren't infallible."

"You know very well my secretary can call me, Mike." The fact was that he didn't want her to go, even resented her going. Not only because of the project, but because of himself. It was a damned juvenile reaction, she decided.

"But *why*, Lisa? That's what I want to know. You told me they've had no news. What can you do that the whole police department, a private eye and your ex-husband can't do?"

"I don't know, exactly," she confessed uneasily. "But I'm her *mother*, Mike. I'm the one who'll be able to figure out where she is, if anyone can. And I can't sit here doing nothing while she may be..." Lisa stopped, unwilling to go on.

"That's illogical, honey. I'd hardly call it 'sitting' here when you're working like a demon, when you're such a vital part of the project. Anyway, if you're the one to figure it out, why can't you do it here?"

"It's not something I can explain," she persisted. "It's just that...I'll feel better, being there. Somehow I think I'll be able to answer all the questions there, in the city where she is. Not here, halfway across the country."

"You said a couple of times that 'here' had become 'home' because of me." She could hear the pain and jealousy in his voice, but she was no longer in the mood to watch her words or keep her temper.

"What you're saying is that you want me here for yourself, not just for the project," she blurted.

"Damned right I do. I never said otherwise, lady. You were the one, remember, who thought I was trying to 'seduce' you into the project."

The discussion had shot off wildly now in all directions, the way quarrels so often do. But she was so exasperated that she couldn't stop it or herself. "Why are you bringing up all these irrelevant things?" she demanded. "The point is that my child is missing and I'm doing nothing whatsoever about it."

"Your *child?*" he repeated wryly. "A seventeen-year-old woman with a lethal ability to manipulate her mommy and foul up a multimillion-dollar job? Some child." Now he looked furious. "And since when am I 'irrelevant'?" he demanded.

But Lisa was furious, too. "I might have known you'd bring up the *cost* of something," she said rashly.

He sat up in bed now, throwing the covers back. "Doctor, there's a cost to this thing that has nothing to do with money. You cost me more misery than the national debt when you keep putting me in second place like this."

He got up, putting out his cigarette with a savage gesture. "I'm going to sleep in the other bedroom now, if you'll excuse me." His voice was hard with anger. "I've got to get up at the crack of dawn, and I have a hell of a day tomorrow. So do you...especially if you're going through with this idiotic trip. So I suggest you get some sleep, too."

"Mike..." But he was striding out of the room. She heard the door to the other bedroom shut with a painful finality.

She turned out the light and lay back, lonely in the wide bed without his consoling presence, feeling the hot, salty tears scald her eyes and begin to flow.

She wanted desperately to go to him, to apologize, to make things right again. But she just couldn't. Let him come to me, she thought obstinately.

But her obstinacy was a cold companion while she lay awake crying, and after the weeping was over, all she was left with was a cold, heavy ache that began in her throat and breast and crept throughout her body.

Lisa still couldn't believe that they had let two nights and one whole day go by without coming to any reconciliation; it was only when the cab was approaching West Twelfth Street that she realized it in full, realized it with a feeling of calm despair.

Everything had been a positive nightmare since Wednesday night, when she had lain awake so long, half hoping for a sound from the other bedroom that would signal the start of their making up. Finally she'd fallen asleep from sheer exhaustion, then slept later than she'd wanted to the next morning.

Mike was gone when she woke. Without even stopping for breakfast she'd dashed to the copter site and just caught one; then she had plunged into a backbreaking load of work at the center, hearing nothing from Mike all day. She worked until eleven Thursday night, her neck and back and shoulders a mass of aches from tension, pressure and effort. Finally she had been satisfied that she had gotten her part of the project in decent enough shape so that it could be turned over to the disapproving Heinz.

Half-asleep, she had been driven back to Houston in a hired car, but she'd still had to pack and wash her hair before she could think of sleeping. And her plane was leaving early the next morning. She was so overtired at that point, so upset over the quarrel with Mike, that she hadn't been able to fall asleep when she finally got the chance. Besides the quarrel, there was also the inevitable guilt over leaving at this particular time, and the very real fear that her departure might prejudice the board against her in the assignment of personnel for the next shuttle flight.

On the plane she'd decided, well, so be it. A woman can't have a child and just waltz away in times of crisis. That's life. It's bitter, but it's true.

Now, as the cab pulled to a stop, Lisa was overcome with a numbing depression. She almost started crying again when she saw the door to her house. It was impossible not to recall that first incredible night with Mike, when he'd kissed her right here on this street. At least, she thought sourly, Brenda's at work. She would be spared the effort of making a cheery greeting when she didn't feel like speaking to a soul.

The cab driver, apparently impressed by her look of sadness and exhaustion, made a gesture rare in his hard-bitten urban kind and actually took her heavy suitcase to her door for her. The unexpected courtesy moved her to tears again, and she tipped him outrageously and let herself into the house.

She breathed a deep sigh of relief. Depressed as she was, it was good to be in the house again, to relax in its shining order and casual beauty. For a minute or two she just walked around the living room and let serenity flow back into her body.

She took off her high-heeled shoes and padded into the kitchen to make herself some food and coffee. After she'd had them she began to feel much better.

It would be heavenly just to go to sleep, she thought, but there was too much to do first. She wanted to get in touch with Jack, and also see the police.

An uninvited picture of Mike flashed before her. It hurt so much that she balled her hands into fists to keep from weeping. Her nails dug into her palms. She realized what she was doing and cut short the silly, masochistic exercise.

After pouring herself another cup of reviving coffee, she called Jack at the hotel where he was staying and was told he was out. With frustrated weariness, she wondered if the police would be out, too. But of course when she called the precinct Jack had referred her to, she was told that the officer concerned would be able to see her that afternoon.

She changed her dress as a psychological refresher and repaired her makeup, appearing at the police station at the appointed time. The officer, while very polite and patient, could not quite conceal an impression of here-we-go-again, confronting the mother of a missing teenager. When she pursued the matter a bit sharply, he told her wearily that his own eighteen-year-old daughter had been missing for the last four years, having run away when she was fourteen.

"Those are the times we're living in, Dr. Heron," he said resignedly.

Lisa left the police station feeling more harassed and impotent than ever.

The only silver lining was the chance to take a brief nap and put her things away before bathing and changing again into a blessedly comfortable pajama suit before Brenda came home from work.

Her friend embraced her warmly, took over dinner preparations with firm efficiency and mixed Lisa a drink. After dinner Brenda made her sit down in the kitchen while she tidied up, and then they had a long, long talk about the whole affair.

It was painful not to be able to tell Brenda about Mike, but Lisa just couldn't at that point. She knew that if she did, she'd dissolve into tears again. It wasn't more than ten o'clock when exhaustion overcame her.

"Please...go to bed," Brenda insisted.

There was no point in not doing so, Lisa judged. She'd talked to Jack, who'd told her that nothing was new. She hadn't called her parents yet. Her mother might be naive enough to swallow the tale that Lisa was shopping with Charlie for school, "taking a breather." Her father wouldn't be...ever. Now that he was in touch with Mike he'd know damned well that only an emergency could have brought Lisa back to

New York. And that would give the whole game away. Not only was Lisa hesitant to upset her mother, but she couldn't predict what effect the news might have on her recuperating father. She prayed that if her father spoke to Mike on the phone, he wouldn't ask for her.

"Why not?" Lisa retorted, so tired that her words were slurred, although she'd had only one cocktail and pots of coffee.

"You poor thing, you look like you're about to drop," Brenda commented kindly.

You don't know the half of it, Lisa retorted in silence, wishing she could tell her friend everything.

"Look, give me a minute and I'll get my stuff out of your way. You ought to have your own room back," Brenda suggested.

Lisa said she wouldn't think of it, that she'd use Charlie's room. She'd already put her things in there earlier.

But then, she reflected, as she went into her daughter's room that night, she hadn't really stopped to look around. Now the sight of Charlie's things was just too much for Lisa.

She lay down on Charlie's bed and burst out crying. She hoped Brenda didn't hear her, but even if she did, she'd be too tactful to intrude. Lisa was overwhelmed with an agonizing loneliness, and she gave herself up to memories of her times with Mike. She'd been trying to dismiss them from her mind for the past two days, but they were too strong for her. So let them come, she thought somberly.

With the strangest combination of pleasure and pain she reviewed the few incredible weeks of their acquaintance, from the first sun-filled day, when she had seen him striding onto the terrace, to the last angry night, when even in their alienation she had not ceased to want him, not for a moment.

At the end of it, mingling with her drowsiness, came a dark, despairing realization: maybe it had been only one of those fleeting, magical things that came once in a lifetime to the fortunate, but was not meant to endure. She loved him with all her heart, and always would, as long as she lived. But she couldn't imagine Mike Nesbitt as a surrogate father, a man who could share the life she'd committed herself to.

Oh, yes, they had so many things in common, she reflected with a swift, indrawn breath of pain, but still, it probably hadn't been meant to last.

Yet when she turned out the light, she saw the book she'd absentmindedly placed on the night table with her other paperbacks—the haunting, everpresent *House of Stars*, where she had first read the love story of the Aries man and the Libra woman; the man with the "bright turquoise eyes," whose rising star was "in fatal opposition" to the woman's own.

It was only a little after nine in Houston, and Mike Nesbitt was still on the job. He felt as if he were walking in his sleep; after the big blowup with Lisa, he'd lain awake a long time, finally gotten an hour or two of sleep, and then abruptly awakened. It had been five-thirty in the morning. He'd crept into the other bedroom and seen her curled in deep sleep. The poor kid had been so tired that even when he lightly kissed her she hadn't stirred, and he'd taken off for the center.

All day Thursday, preoccupied as he was, he'd been distracted, feeling like hell. A dozen times he'd started to call her, but he'd remembered the incredible task she'd mapped out for herself and realized that she probably wouldn't be too receptive to an interruption. Then another mess of his own had come up, and by the time he was untangled and called her, there had been no answer.

And he'd been in no shape himself to face another confrontation. He had hoped that she might change her mind, that somehow she would decide to stay. When he had called the hotel, just to say a few words to her, she hadn't come in yet. Then, exhausted, he had gone to sleep in one of the emergency bedrooms at the center.

On Friday morning he'd been rudely awakened by Gould, who told him excitedly that they were getting very near to the resolution of that maddening bug. He had rushed with Gould to the lab, keeping one eye on the time. By the time he had been able to call the hotel, Lisa had left for the airport.

Today there had been hardly a minute to think at all. He was still so sleep-deprived that he could hardly function; it was affecting his judgment. Three times in the past half hour he'd given Gould the wrong readings.

Now Gould said quietly, "I think you'd better take a break, Mike."

"What the hell do you mean, *I'd* better take a break?" He was feeling very belligerent.

"I mean you can't cut it right now. You're not doing any of us any good."

"You sound like Rayburn, man. What is this, anyway?" Mike demanded, feeling foolish even as he spoke, because he knew Gould had a point.

"What's with you, Mike? You're dead on your feet. Why aren't you sleeping at night?"

"I don't want to talk about it," he growled.

"Well, you'd better talk about it to *somebody*, pal, because it's eating you alive and holding up our work," Gould said. "Look, Mike, take a break, for a couple of hours. I'm going to take one, too. It's getting away from us again, and I think we all need to back off a little. See you here about eleven, okay?"

"Okay." Mike nodded and walked out of the lab, thinking, Gould's right, as always. Maybe I *should* talk to somebody.

Heinz?

Mike almost laughed aloud. His opinion of shrinks—except for one, he amended, feeling an odd little pain shoot through his chest—was not high. Heinz was an all-right man, though, and a friend as well as a colleague of Lisa's.

And tell him what, Mike asked himself sardonically. He wandered out of the building in an aimless way, passing the security man. The man relaxed when he recognized Nesbitt.

Mike raised his hand, nodded and passed. He took a deep breath of the warm, heavy air. It had the feel of an approaching storm. Mike walked on past the green oval that was almost black now in the semidark, catching sight of the giant rockets alongside the parking lots.

Tell Heinz what, he asked himself again. That he'd reacted like a spoiled, self-centered kid, throwing a tantrum because Lisa was concerned about her daughter? And have Heinz agree?

Hell, no. He'd talk to himself for a while, be his own shrink.

Mike found his car and drove off, hardly aware where he was headed, driving with absent competence.

He savored the memories of every hour he'd spent with Lisa Heron, wondering again at the sheer good fortune of their meeting. She was the greatest gift he'd ever been given, the most magnificent woman he'd ever hoped to find.

And he, like a fool, had believed that winning her, making her love him, would be the be-all and the end-all of life. He'd rushed in with the speed of a training jet, without considering that her life, when they met, had already been formed, that she had commitments and responsibilities.

Mike's eyelids felt like lead. He sighted a roadside cafe and braked. Inside he ordered coffee and drank two cups quickly. The other people in the place were blurs; he hardly glanced at the woman who served him. There was a plaintive country song on the juke-box—someone was leaving someone on a one-way train. The image slammed into his consciousness with the force of a blow to his body. She was gone.

But he'd be damned if he'd lose her. Not now, he promised himself. Mike paid for his coffee and checked the clock over the counter. Time he was getting back.

As he sped back to the center, Mike Nesbitt swore that he'd make it up with Lisa if he had to crawl on his belly like a reptile. If they could only get things on the project wrapped up enough, he'd fly to New York in the morning. It would be better not to give her a chance to say no.

He parked and rushed back to the lab.

Gould was pacing up and down. Sighting Mike, he snapped, "Where the hell have you been?"

"What's up?"

"I've been on the phone with Marley, that's all. And he's come up with something new. The guys are already on it. And Marley wants you to call him back." Gould took a small folded sheet of paper from his breast pocket and handed it to Mike.

Mike took the paper, unfolded it and glanced at the number. It was an unfamiliar one. He must have been released, Mike thought. This must be his home phone. It was midnight there.

He hurried to a phone and dialed.

"Mike." Marley's deep voice sounded strong but anxiety-ridden.

"What can I do for you, Mr. Marley?" Mike was puzzled. If Marley had come up with anything else on the disequilibrium, he'd have told Gould.

"You can tell me what's up with Lisa. I didn't want to bring this up before, but I have a feeling you're the one to know, Mike." There was a smile in the voice now. And Mike Nesbitt realized that Marley was a thousand times sharper than he'd figured. Even on the phone he hadn't been able to hide his feeling for Marley's daughter.

"You're right, sir." Mike hesitated. Lisa hadn't wanted to upset her father with the news of Charlie's disappearance. Obviously he still didn't know.

"I called her hotel tonight, and they told me she's flown to New York," Marley went on. "By that time it was so late in New York that I didn't want to call her house and disturb the woman who's staying there. Why did she come back, Mike?"

Mike took a deep breath. There was no way around it now. "Charlie's missing." He dreaded Marley's reaction.

To his relief, the man was calm when he repeated, "Missing?"

Mike told him the whole story, including Lisa's superhuman wrap up of her part of the project before she left.

"That's my daughter." Marley sounded proud, and very much in control when he added, "She's got to stop trying to protect me. I'll see her tomorrow. She's going to need a father's support, Mike. You've got your hands full now, I know. But if you're half the man I think you are, you'll be there for her, too."

"You've got it," Mike said fervently.

"Good. I thought so." Marley spoke with great satisfaction. "Get back to work, Mike. And good luck."

"Thanks, Mr. Marley."

"One more thing. It's 'Phil.'"

Mike felt as if he'd just been awarded the Medal of Honor or something. He grinned. "Thanks, Phil."

Hanging up, he found he was a whole new man. Marley had been very up-front with him, and totally together. That was the best part of all. No, the best part was that Mike Nesbitt had been given Marley's blessing.

Mike went back to work with new enthusiasm. Fourteen hours' straight sleep could not have done more to revive him.

The fire in him flickered a little when they collided with another new problem, then a second, a third and a fourth. On Saturday he debated calling Lisa. He was hungry to hear her voice. What he really wanted was just to show up, take her by surprise, break down her defenses before she had time to build new ones. Give her his support.

But there might be news of Charlie. He called her New York house and Marley's Long Island house three times, never getting an answer. Finally on Saturday night he got Lisa's friend, who told him there was still no news.

Sunday was an unreal day of unremitting work and the quick catnaps that he'd trained himself to take in space.

It wasn't until Sunday evening that they got the problems knocked. A deafening shout went up from the entire crew. "We're there!" Gould yelled at Mike with jubilation.

Mystifying Gould, Mike shouted, "Not just yet!"

Chapter 10

Lisa poured herself a second cup of coffee, glorying in the Monday-morning quiet of her house. She gazed out the kitchen window at the garden. The roses looked even more vivid than usual in the gray, rain-boding light. Perversely she welcomed the coming bad weather; it was just right for her mood.

A long night's uninterrupted sleep had restored her, and her reunion with her father on Saturday had brought her a whole new good feeling, mitigated only by the continuing absence of Charlie...and of Mike.

The thought of them both tugged at her heart and cast a shadow over the relative brightness of her weekend in Long Island.

Saturday morning, as soon as she'd gotten the elated phone call from her father, Lisa had scribbled a note for Brenda, thrown a few things into a small bag and rushed to the Long Island train.

Her father had been standing on the platform when the train drew into the station, and she'd almost leaped into his wide-open arms. She had been incredulous over how well he looked, a strong, tall, masculine version of herself, with his wise dark eyes and silvery hair still thick and vital.

She'd told him without exaggeration that he looked like her older brother, and he had teased her for flattering him. They'd had so much to say to each other that they'd arrived at the house before she even noticed.

At the last moment he'd asked her not to mention the matter of Charlie to her mother, saying he preferred to wait until they could tell her good news. Lisa had been uncertain, but her father had said, to remind her, "She's become very fragile, you know, after all that happened with...me."

"And me," Lisa had said generously, reluctant to let him dwell on any guilt-provoking thoughts. "She was really upset about the divorce." And she had agreed that they would be silent a bit longer. Belatedly she'd realized that it hadn't been necessary to protect her father from the news; he seemed stronger now than he had ever been.

Her mother had greeted Lisa with affection, remarking that she looked a little thin, and reproaching her for working so hard. This had led to the suggestion that they spend the afternoon on their boat. Lisa had hedged, wanting to be near a phone in case she got some news, but she could hardly refuse, since this was one of her favorite recreations and she didn't want her mother to suspect anything.

Moreover her father had told her in a private moment that she could check in with Brenda and Jack at intervals throughout the afternoon, and Lisa had to admit to herself that the hours in the sun had loosened many of the knots in her tense body. When they had docked and gone home to change for dinner, Lisa had checked with Jack and Brenda again, but there had been nothing new.

She had made herself appear as gay and relaxed as she could at a long, festive dinner with her parents' friends. Enervated by the emotions of the happy reunion, soothed by the day in the sun and champagne at dinner, she had slept a little better that night.

Lisa had come back to New York Sunday night, and found a note from Brenda: "Mike Nesbitt called from Houston late last night." She had gone to bed in a state of new confusion.

Now, sitting at the breakfast table late on Monday morning, she wondered what the reason had been for his call. The meticulous Brenda would have given her any special message, so what Lisa had gotten was obviously all there was.

Something else was puzzling her. Her father had had a mysterious, almost conspiratorial, air all weekend. What had that been about?

She recoiled at the sudden ringing of the phone. Snapping to alertness, she raced to answer it.

"Lisa!" It was her father. "They've licked it. I just got a call from Gould in Houston."

"Oh, Dad, that's fabulous," she said, but she felt a strange sense of anticlimax. Gould had called him; not Mike. Where was he? What was he doing right now? Her heart ached. Now Mike *and* Charlie were missing.

But she gathered her wandering thoughts. Her father was asking if she'd had any more news of Charlie, and she was answering, then listening to her father's exuberant report about the project. She congratulated him again before they discussed Charlie's situation one more time.

When they hung up Lisa took another cup of coffee into the peaceful living room. She picked up the newspaper that was delivered to the house each morning. It showed signs of having been read and then neatly reassembled for her by Brenda.

Lisa sat down and looked through it idly, amazed at her own bland reaction to the success of the project, even when she read a sketchy report of it in the paper. Naturally it was too soon for all the news to come through, and much of it was classified anyway.

It did little for her morale even when she read about her own part in the project and saw Heinz's glowing comments on Dr. Lisa Heron's expertise. She felt so disconnected from it all now, alone in the world without Mike, without Charlie. And she had a gloomy feeling that now she'd be the last woman to be chosen for a flight, after her untimely departure for New York. She could just imagine what someone like Rayburn would make of that.

But even if it had been her swan song, her one and only almost-adventure into space, the fact remained that her daughter had still not been found, and she couldn't waste another minute brooding on other matters.

With absent dejection, she leafed on through the paper, hardly knowing what she read. But then she turned a page back abruptly, with a loud snap.

There it was—the announcement of an event that would be irresistible to Charlie, one she couldn't stay away from, especially if she was already in Manhattan. And it would be held at two-thirty this afternoon.

Lisa went to the phone and called her father. When she told him what she had in mind, he said triumphantly, "To quote Professor Higgins, 'I think she's got it.' I'll meet you there at two, my dear. And if I read my starry grandkid right, we'll have company."

As she hung up, Lisa thought that his timing was just right. Charlie was a last-minute arriver. She'd probably rush around the exhibits and take her seat as the program was starting. They might even meet her at the door.

Lisa had a whole new outlook on everything. Now she felt driven by wild optimism. She rushed around tidying up the house, checked the refrigerator and decided to run out and stock up on items Charlie liked. Then she called Heinz in Houston to check on the progress of their end of the project and was heartened by his report.

It was already eleven, she saw, and she told herself that she'd better move. She slung on some casual clothes, food-shopped and bought some new candles. Passing a boutique on Greenwich Avenue, she saw a crocheted summer sweater in a delicious shade of lilac that was pure Charlie. Lisa bought it and had it gift-wrapped. The store's yellow-and-white gift wrapping was so attractive that Lisa impulsively decided to buy some yellow roses from an outdoor display; then as an act of faith in a celebration, stopped and picked up party items in sunny yellow.

Despite being laden with her heavy shopping bags, she practically floated down the short block to Sixth Avenue, where she looked up at the wonderful witch's castle that housed the library.

After she had stowed everything away and put the gift-wrapped package on the coffee table, she arranged the roses and put the fresh yellow candles into their crystal holders. It was twelve-thirty already, and she had no idea of how bad the traffic would be. In record time she showered, washed and blew dry her hair, then looked out the bedroom window.

A pale, watery sun was struggling through the gray light; the air was heavy with humidity, half promising a storm. She got into a cool, pale pink dress and after a second's debate, slipped the twinkling stars, with milky opal centers, into her ears. Why not, she reflected. The stars might symbolize a magic interval that was gone forever, but she would wear them from now on anyway. She was entitled to a memory, after all. And besides, the stars signified more than her love for Mike Nesbitt: they stood for her everlasting passion for the conquest of unknown space, and for Charlie's intense delight in the meaning of the heaven's patterns.

And what could be more appropriate for today's destination?

Lisa hurried out and was elated to find an empty taxi at the corner of Sixth Avenue. As they made the rattling journey uptown, Lisa kept looking nervously at her watch, hoping against hope that the traffic would cooperate this once, wondering if she should have taken the subway.

To her relief, however, it was only ten minutes to two when the cab braked abruptly near the Planetarium. She saw her father standing outside, his light summer suit jacket slung over his broad shoulder. The sun was out again.

Lisa thrust the fare at the driver and jumped from the cab, hurrying toward her father.

He was smiling and waving. As she got nearer, he called out, "Slow down. It's too hot to run." He hugged her and kissed her on the cheek. "What a day!"

"Any sign yet?" she asked eagerly.

"Not yet. I looked in and there was just the usual starry crowd." He chuckled, but it was a nervous laugh; Lisa could tell he was as wired-up as she was. "A number of elderly ladies in mauve," he went on, his tension reflected in his uncharacteristic chatter, "and a bunch of those horribly earnest, sweaty young women dressed like fruit pickers."

Lisa responded with a nervous laugh of her own. "Let's go."

They stepped from the hot, heavy air into the relative coolness of the Planetarium. A large crowd was milling about among some new exhibits; others were already entering the auditorium marked by a sign: Astrologers, the First Astronomers.

Lisa glanced aside at her father. His dark eyes darted everywhere, and he made another comment, as if to release more of his tension. "I can't wait to hear what these astronomers will make of Charlie's favorite subject."

Lisa was too tightly wound now even to answer. She felt a hard knot in her throat. Her heart was hammering, and her palms were uncomfortably clammy and cold at once.

Phil Marley glanced at his watch. "We have time," he said. "Let's check out the rest of the exhibits." Their investigation yielded nothing. It was almost time for the lecture to begin.

"We'd better go on in, honey." Lisa's father touched her elbow.

She nodded, too stricken to answer. They must have been wrong, after all. She waited numbly while her father submitted their tickets and then preceded him into the big auditorium, already dimmed for the presentation. There was an eerie, silvery light over everything under the awesome, wheeling replicas of the celestial worlds with their planets and stars.

Lisa and her father took seats on the aisle near the back, where they could see everyone who came in. "You take this side," he whispered, "and I'll take that one."

Lisa just nodded again. She was losing hope now.

The program began. A hidden lecturer, deep-voiced, declaimed over loudspeakers, "The significance which early man attached to the movements of the sun and moon, the planets and the stars, remains in the great megaliths of Western Europe..."

Lisa tuned out, vaguely aware of references to Stonehenge and the astrology of the Mayans, while she watched the latest arrivals.

The voice went on, speaking of Egyptian and Oriental astrology, beginning to touch on the Middle Ages when Lisa saw a familiar figure hurrying down the aisle.

It was Charlie. She'd know that floating golden hair, that vital, upright carriage, anywhere.

Her father stiffened to attention and touched her arm. Lisa started to rise. "Wait," her father whispered.

"Wait?" Lisa found she'd spoken aloud. Someone shushed her.

"Yes," he whispered. "Let her see the show. She won't be going anywhere." Lisa stared at him in the silvery light. His dark, wise eyes gleamed at her as he smiled.

"All right," she agreed in a whisper. Her father knew what he was doing, as always. Charlie would be in a much more receptive mood after this brief visit to her country of the stars.

Lisa stared at the back of her daughter's golden head, saw her raise her face to stare, enchanted, at the wheeling constellations in the blue-black space. Her daughter's expression was deeply touching, and Lisa felt as if her own attention was captured and held by this ancient magic. Perhaps, she decided, she'd been too busy being a practical mother to share in her daughter's dreams. And too much a mother, she added with painful insight, to share *Mike's* dreams, either...and to pursue the dream that had been her own for years, even before she knew him.

Once again she was astonished at her father's sensitive intelligence. After all the strain and worry, after all their hard work and pressure, all three of them needed this show. She glimpsed her father's face; he looked as young as Charlie.

By the time intermission was announced Lisa was feeling a wonderful new calm, a profound conviction that everything would come right.

The audience was standing up. Lisa and her father moved aside to let people pass, never losing sight of Charlie, then stepped back to wait for her to reach their place.

When she did, Phil Marley called out softly, "Charlie."

She stopped, transfixed, catching sight of her grandfather, then Lisa. "Oh, Mother!"

Charlie rushed to Lisa and hugged her close. "Mother." Then she let Lisa go and moved to her grandfather. They were holding up traffic in the worst way, hearing various people say irritably, "Excuse *me*.... Do you *mind*?...Well, *really*."

In a happy tangle they made their way to the door; Charlie was bubbling with giddy laughter and, overwhelmed with tenderness and exasperation, with anger and relief and love, Lisa found herself infected by it, too.

At last they found some breathing room in the lobby. For a moment they just stood there, looking at each other. Finally Charlie blurted, "I'm so sorry, Ma. I'm so sorry." She began to cry.

Lisa took Charlie in her arms, saying, "Hush, now. Hush. It's fine now. Everything's fine." In the midst of it all, she couldn't help thinking, everything except me. A vivid image of Mike Nesbitt flashed before her inner eye. She shook her head, as if to clear it of that vision, and added soberly, "It's just that you gave us an awful fright. We didn't know whether you were dead or alive, Charlie."

"I know." Charlie sniffed, and Lisa rummaged in her bag for a tissue and handed it to her daughter. "Thanks." Charlie gave her a shaky smile.

"Where have you been?" Phil Marley demanded gently.

"In a hotel, in midtown." Good heavens, that was why they couldn't find her. "In a place where I didn't know a soul. I felt like I just had to...get away from everything for a while, think everything out. I...read some books that told me what a jerk I'd been about you and Mike."

Marley raised his brows and exchanged a glance with Lisa.

"You don't have to worry about that anymore," Lisa said quietly, struggling to keep her voice even and calm. "That's over, Charlie."

"I don't think so, my dear." Lisa saw her father looking toward the entrance of the building, to which her own back was turned. "I don't think so at all." Her father was grinning from ear to ear.

Lisa wheeled. Mike Nesbitt, resplendent in his summer dress uniform, looking bigger and taller, more dashing and tanned, than ever, was coming toward them with long, triumphant strides.

Mike and Lisa wandered slowly out of Harbin's after their late supper. The waiters were already blowing out the votive candles in their tulip-shaped crystal holders atop the pale pink cloths that matched Lisa's cool dress. But the small trees outside were still shining with their myriad white bulbs like tiny constellations. Mike stopped Lisa with a gentle pressure of his fingers.

"Wait a minute." They stood looking at the lights. "Lisa, I'll never forget, even when I'm an old, old man, what you said about these little trees. That when you saw me standing in front of them that first night I seemed to be walking in space, among the stars."

She turned and gazed up at him. His bright blue eyes were blazing with a deeper tenderness than she'd ever seen in them before, and she raised herself on her toes to kiss him. They held each other for an instant on the half-deserted street.

"Let's walk a little," she suggested. "Revisit the scene of the crime."

"The sweetest crime ever perpetrated, Doctor." They walked slowly to Washington Square and stood under the arch, listening to the summer sounds of laughter, love songs from transistors, plucked guitars.

"Oh, listen," Lisa said breathlessly. They caught the ripple of mandolins playing a soulful Italian air.

"It's the neighborhood troubadors," Lisa explained, smiling. "They were playing here on that first night." Mike's arm tightened around her waist. He drew her closer to him, and they walked in dreamy unison back through the arch, looking up the tree-framed, light-filled vista of Fifth Avenue.

As they strolled up Fifth past the mews in close, dazzled silence, Lisa felt an incredible joy, an over-powering peace. Swiftly she reviewed the incredible, festive day.

After a few warm words with Mike, Phil Marley had taken Charlie back to the lecture. Mike and Lisa had gone outside to sit on a bench under the trees.

Indifferent to the passersby, he had raised her hands to his lips and kissed them. "I heard what your father said, Lisa. He's right. It's far from over for me; for me it's only beginning."

And she had known that it was just beginning for her, as well. They had so much to say that the others had been back with them again before they had even started.

The whole day had been turned around. The brooding, pale light and the oppressive humidity were swept away by a refreshing wind that told them the storm had passed over, and the sun had shone with unseasonable gentleness. Lisa felt that the entire universe had been renewed in two swift hours. Suddenly all of them had been talking at once, improvising the rest of the afternoon, friendly, warm and utterly companionable. Phil Marley had told them that Lisa's mother was coming in to join them for dinner, and that he'd asked her to meet them at the house.

"That's perfect!" Lisa said. "I was planning a celebration."

"I like that," Mike commented with admiration. "You're an eternal optimist. Well, so am I," he added with deep significance, making everyone laugh when he leered at Lisa.

With serendipity they found a big, old-fashioned taxi with jump seats and took it down to the Village. Brenda had come home; she rushed to Charlie and embraced her. And the party began.

Lisa's mother arrived, too happy to reproach Marley very much for keeping her in the dark about Charlie. Mike dashed around the corner, returning with vintage champagne, and the women got the party together. Everyone was too excited to think of a full-scale dinner, so they feasted on the party food, which was ample.

Later, while Mike talked to the Marleys, Brenda and Lisa conferred about arrangements; Lisa insisted that Brenda stay on. Charlie would be going back to the Cape the next day, and Lisa said wickedly that she would make other arrangements. Then Lisa and Charlie had a nice, long talk in Charlie's room.

"You know, Ma," Charlie had confided, "I think I'm starting to learn how to let go."

Lisa hugged her. "I've had to learn a bit myself about letting go. I think it's high time for both of us."

"Speaking of which," Charlie retorted, "is it okay if I go out tonight? I called a friend this afternoon."

"It's positively A-Okay. Don't wait up for me, either. We'll have the rest of our talk tomorrow," Lisa promised.

Charlie laughed. "Wait up for you tonight? No way...no way in the world."

Then Brenda and Charlie had gone out on their dates, the Marleys had returned to Long Island, and somewhere along the way Mike and Lisa had gone to Harbin's for their small late supper.

Now, strolling up Fifth at his side, Lisa felt as light as a balloon. When they reached Eleventh Street, she said, "Let's cross over. I want to show you something. Something that made me cry the other day, when I thought...well, when I was alone. And I want to see it now with you, when I'm so happy."

"Your wish is always my command," he agreed, taking her hand in his. They crossed Fifth Avenue, and she led him to the wooden fence outside the church at Eleventh Street, where some high-hearted woman had neatly written the most delightful graffiti Lisa had ever seen in New York. In a flowing hand, in white, all along the fence, were the words: "Walking to Fifth Avenue she smiled, thinking of her dearest love. When she reached the corner something lovely and small blossomed inside her. At the office she filed this carefully under *'Si, corazon.'* Yes, my heart, yes."

Mike read it swiftly, grinning. "It's wonderful," he said softly. "File this under 'Forever, Lisa Heron.' He took her in his arms and kissed her hungrily, and she could feel the deep intensity of his longing.

"Oh, Lisa, I can't wait for tomorrow...."

She knew then what he was saying; he had accepted the idea that they would have to spend this night apart. She was profoundly moved by his sweetness, his consideration. He had taken it for granted that she would want to stay in the house tonight with Charlie. This was a new Mike Nesbitt.

But it was also a new Lisa Heron. She was never going to spend another night away from him again. And she said so. He stared at her, speechless, and his eyes reflected an even greater happiness.

"Lisa...do you mean it?"

"Oh, yes. This is a new regime, Colonel. My daughter has gladly given me a key to the door," she teased him.

He was speechless with happiness; all he could do was stare down at her, then draw her closer to him as they walked slowly around the corner up Fifth Avenue, past the bright green yard that bordered the lovely church of gray weathered stone. Across the street, on either side of the entrance doors to the venerable Salmagundi Club, someone had affixed bright blue, pink, orange and yellow balloons.

"Oh, look, look!" she said. "That's just what I feel like—balloons, all bright-colored and floating."

"So do I—*free*-floating, Doctor. And while we're on the subject of space, I have a lot more to tell you. A whole lot more." He chuckled. "You know, now that the...urgency is gone from saying good-night..."

She laughed, making a wicked face.

"...we seem to have worlds of time," he concluded.

"We do indeed. So I'll just stop by the house and give it a quick check, then we can have that talk, before we take off for...somewhere."

"My readings make it two distant, light-year-long blocks," he kidded, "to my hotel at Fifth and Tenth Street. That should be nice and near, and give you an early start tomorrow with...our daughter."

Our daughter, he'd said. That one small phrase brought her a new gladness; it carried so much with it: the willingness to share her responsibilities with her; the depth of his commitment. Lisa was so overwhelmed that she could thank him only with her upturned look. His expression was ineffably tender in the golden lamplight of the empty street.

She let them quietly into the narrow red-brick house. It was very still. There was a note on the console table.

Mike looked around the hall and smiled. "I love your house," he whispered. As Lisa picked up the note, he put his arms around her from behind.

"This is from Brenda," she said. "Evidently both the tenants are tucked away. Early dates." She reveled in the feeling of his encircling arms and leaned back. He kissed the top of her head.

"Would you like some coffee before we go?"

"Very much. I've got a lot to tell you, lady. An awful lot that escaped me before," he chuckled softly, "in all the excitement."

They wandered into the kitchen, and he sat down at the table, first surveying the pleasant room with its pale wood paneling, turquoise and dark red touches and shining copper implements. Then he watched Lisa prepare the coffee.

Neither of them said another word until it was ready, just smiled at each other in a buzz of tipsy happiness. Lisa poured their coffee and handed him his; then, before she sat down, she stood for a moment behind his chair, planting a light kiss on the top of his head, caressing his ears delicately with her fingers. He made a sound of deep content, reacting with instant sensitivity to her touch.

"Knock, knock." It was Charlie's feisty voice.

She was standing at the door, grinning, in a short robe.

Without moving, Lisa said, "Hello, there," smiling at her.

Charlie came in and sat down. "Want some coffee?" Lisa offered.

"No, thanks. I'm just passing through. I came to see you, Mike. I never thanked you for the window."

"The window?" He was puzzled.

"From the store in Washington. Bett told me that's what it was," she added to Lisa. To Mike she explained. "My stepmother's a fashion nut. She recognized it right away. Anyway, I wanted to tell you it's the greatest."

Mike smiled. "I'm glad you liked it."

Before Lisa sat down, she went to Charlie and ruffled her hair. "Did you know that I got a window, too?"

"My gosh!" Charlie's brows swooped upward, and she looked at Mike again. "You know, you're *neat*."

"I've got something else neat for you both," Mike said exuberantly. "Your mother's going into space...very soon."

Charlie shrieked, "What?" and Lisa gasped.

"Mike...do you mean it?"

"Damned right. It should be about November. You'll be a mission specialist on my flight—that is, if you're interested." He gave Lisa a mischievous look.

"*Interested?* Oh, Mike."

"And you'll never guess what the project's been named...Project Athena. For the goddess. The lady of wisdom and courage."

Lisa couldn't believe it for a minute; it all seemed too good to be true. Charlie was so flabbergasted that she was just sitting there, staring at them both.

"There's just one minor problem..." Mike began.

I knew it, Lisa thought. There had to be something.

"I don't know how we're going to list you," he said to Lisa. "As Heron...or Nesbitt. You haven't told me. What do you think, Charlie?"

Lisa knew exactly what he was doing. His light, teasing intonation could not hide his anxiety, his seriousness; he was looking at Charlie with pleading in his eyes.

Charlie knew it, too. She was smiling, but her answer was serious. "I think Nesbitt sounds better."

Lisa leaned over and caressed her daughter's face with her hand, blinking back the sudden tears in her eyes. Charlie kissed her mother's fingers, then leaped up and went to Mike, giving him a quick kiss on the cheek. Her look of happiness warmed Lisa's heart.

"Congratulations, astronauts," Charlie declared. "Now I'm going to bed." She went swiftly out, and Lisa heard the faint sound of her bare feet skimming up the stairs.

She looked back at Mike. "Well...you have my daughter's okay. Don't tell me you also got my father's."

"Of course." So that, she thought, was the meaning of her father's conspiratorial looks all weekend.

"I see. You asked everyone, it seems, but you forgot to check back with me." She was trying for sternness, but it wasn't working very well, and he knew it. He grinned widely.

"Oh, I knew I'd get around to that." Then his smile faded abruptly, and his whole face took on the sober, pleading expression it had worn when he'd spoken to Charlie. "Will you, Lisa? Will you please marry me? Tell me that you will and put me out of my misery."

"Yes, Mike Nesbitt. Yes. I can't imagine it any other way," she said softly, with equal seriousness. His eyes were bright; his smiling mouth and every feature of his face, even the posture of his body, expressed his relief, his happiness.

"Then you'd better take this," he said in a shaky voice, reaching into his breast pocket. "You'll need something to wear for the night." He stretched his fist across the table. She held her hand out palm upwards, and he opened his fingers. A ring fell on her palm.

She exclaimed and looked at it. It was a glittering dome of many small, fine diamonds. In the gentle light the ring twinkled like a tiny constellation.

He took it from her palm and slipped it on the fourth finger of her left hand. "Stars for your hand," he murmured, "to match the ones in your eyes...and at your ears. Lady, I'm going to cover you with stars before we're done."

"You already have, Colonel." She felt that she was living in a dream from which she'd never waken.

He reached out both his hands and captured hers. "You know, I have so much to tell you still...about the flight, and everything. The fact—which makes me very proud—that I wasn't even the one who recommended you. I didn't have to. The powers that be were so impressed with the job you did that all *I* had to do was approve."

She was amazed at that, but waited for him to go on.

"Yes," he said, "there's an awful lot left to tell you. But I have a feeling you won't mind if we wait."

"My darling, I won't mind at all." She gave him a meaningful smile and got to her feet. Taking his cue, he followed her into the hall. She got a small overnight bag from the closet.

His eyes glinted with pleased amusement.

"So it's all go then," he stage-whispered, "for orbital coast, and a nice, sweet trajectory? Do you read me, Doctor?"

"I read you, Colonel."

He gave her one last big, strong hug and a gentle kiss before she shut the closet door again and, with a swift glance around, turned out the light and stepped out the door.

Mike took her bag from her hand on the stoop. Then, glancing across the street, he said, "Look!"

Just opposite them a bouquet of many colored balloons was tied to the grilled metal gate of a neighbor's basement entrance. "The whole city's celebrating us," Mike commented, putting his arm around her.

They started east, matching their slow steps to each other's, and she responded, "That's only appropriate. This is a momentous occasion—the blending of 'fatal opposites.'"

Feeling his hand tighten around her waist, Lisa recalled the delightful book of stars, and the love story of the Libra woman and the Aries man whose voice was "hard and bright, like the trumpets," whose eyes burned like turquoise fire in his tanned, reckless face.

When she looked up at Mike she saw that face above her. And they were no longer walking along a city street on the planet earth; they were moving on another plane through alien gravity toward a world she'd never known, could still hardly imagine.

Up there, in an uncharted sky, their star was rising.